WHERE
RAINBOW ENDS

A Play

by

CLIFFORD MILLS and JOHN RAMSAY

With Music

by

ROGER QUILTER

Revised Version

by

EVELYN SHILLINGTON

SAMUEL FRENCH

LONDON

NEW YORK SYDNEY TORONTO HOLLYWOOD

Secretaries of dramatic societies wishing to arrange for production of *Where the Rainbow Ends* by amateurs must make application to—

Messrs Samuel French Ltd
26 Southampton Street
Strand, London, WC2E 7JE

or their authorized agents, giving the following particulars—

1. The name of the town and theatre or hall in which it is proposed to give the production.

2. The maximum seating capacity of the place of performance.

3. The number of performances it is intended to give.

Upon receipt of these particulars, Messrs Samuel French Ltd will quote the terms upon which a licence for performance will be granted.

The Piano score and band parts are available on hire.

The costumes and wigs used in the production of the play may be obtained from Messrs Charles Fox Ltd, 25 Shelton Street, London, WC2H 9HX.

ISBN 0 573 15021 5

Printed in Great Britain by W & J Mackay Limited, Chatham

CHARACTERS

MORTALS

Rosamund Carey, a child
Crispian Carey, her brother
Matilda Flint, their aunt
Joseph Flint, her brother
Monsieur Bertrand, a curio dealer
William, the "Boots"
Jim Blunders, Crispian's friend
Betty Blunders, his sister
John Carey, Rosamund and Crispian's father
Vera Carey, his wife
Cubs, a baby lion

IMMORTALS

Speaking

St George
The Dragon King
Dunks, his chief minister
The Genie of the Carpet
Will-o'-the-Wisp
The Sea Witch
The Slacker

Non-speaking

The Woodmouse
The Fairy Queen
The Black Bear
1st Elf
2nd Elf
The Slitherslime
The Spirit of the Lake
1st Green Dragon
2nd Green Dragon
1st Red Dragon
2nd Red Dragon

Rabbits, Elves, Fairies, Frogs, Hyenas, Dragon-flies, Green Dragons, Red Dragons, Rainbow Children

SYNOPSIS OF SCENES

WHERE THE RAINBOW ENDS

ACT I

The library at "Riverside", Maidenhead. Early evening

The house was the home of the late Professor Carey, a renowned Persian scholar. The library is a large, handsomely furnished room, lined with well-filled bookcases, with many curios collected by the late owner. French window C of the back wall lead into the garden, with a view of the River Thames in the distance. A door up L leads to the entrance hall, and a door down R to a passage and thence to the dining-room. The fireplace is L. There is a small concealed gap in the scenery above the door down R which is used to facilitate the removal of St George's cloak. A table, with a large cloth on it, stands LC with a chair above it. On the table is a piece of rope, some tie-on labels and on the floor is a packet of pins. A small table stands up R. A set of library steps stands RC. Near bookcase up R are two packing cases, with lids on. Over the fireplace is a portrait of an elderly gentleman, with a scholarly, kindly face. The floor is carpeted and a large Persian mat lies on the floor in front of the french windows. There is a smaller rug by the fireplace. Other furniture, as dressing, may be added at the discretion of the producer. There is a table-lamp on the table LC and a light pendant C controlled by switches above the door R

When the CURTAIN *rises Rosamund Carey is seated on the library steps. She is a pretty girl about fourteen. She has a book in her hands and there is a gap in the bookshelves R from where she has extracted it. The room is lit by the light of the table-lamp on the table LC and the bright glow of the fire. The french windows and curtains are open, the door down R is closed and the door up L is open*

Rosamund (*reading*) "Now whosoever shall read this book whose faith is 1
strong and heart pure, will find ere they close its pages the way to the
land where the rainbow ends. There blooms the flower of happiness
which grows in no other clime, and here all lost loved ones are found."
(*She looks up and repeats with ecstasy*) "*All lost loved ones are found!*"
(*She reads*)
"Now all who would reach this fair land must first pass through the
dread country of the Dragon, which bars the way—and herein many
perils and dangers are encountered. Happy are they who early find
Faith's Magic Carpet to bear then safely on their way—yet even so . . ."

The sound of a commotion is heard off up L. *Rosamund jumps off the steps, runs to the light switch above the door down* R *and switches on the centre light*

Crispian (*off* L) You brute! Leave off!

Crispian Carey enters up L. *He holds William, the bell-boy by the collar and drags him on with him. Crispian is a nice-looking boy aged about fifteen. He wears a school blazer*

(*as he enters*) You brute! (*He drags William to* L *of the table* LC) I'll teach you to kick a dumb animal! (*He shakes William*)

William Let me go! You're 'urting me!

Crispian Serves you right, you coward! (*He throws William down* L *then moves to door up* L *and calls*) Come along, Cubs, old chap. (*He moves* C)

Cubs, a baby lion, enters up L. *He wears a collar with red, white and blue ribbon (these ribbons are separate). He looks askance at William and growls holding up an injured paw. Then runs affectionately to* R *of Crispian*

Rosamund (*moving to the steps*) Poor darling! (*She puts the book on the steps. To William*) You cruel, horrid boy!

Crispian (*patting Cubs*) Poor old chap. No one shall hurt you while I'm about. (*Looks towards table up* R) Let's give him some Lion-cub Mixture, Rosamund. That'll do him good.

Rosamund Of course! (*moves to table up* R *and takes large bottle marked "Lion-cub Mixture" from table, moves to* R *of Cubs and hands bottle to Crispian*)

Crispian (*to Cubs*) Come on, old chap.

Cubs looks up joyfully, uncorks bottle and tips it into Cub's mouth

This will make you grow a big, strong fellow!

Cubs drinks, then rubs his tummy with delight and crosses to fireplace and lies down on rug

Crispian (*recorks the bottle, hands it to Rosamund, then makes a run at William*) As for you, you little squirt . . .

William dodges up L *of the table* LC. *Rosamund replaces the bottle on table up* R

Crispian (*chasing William*) You be off, and if I catch you at it again I'll give you something to cry for!

William (*snivelling*) I'll be even with you yet. I'll tell the mistress what you've done. 'Oo do you think you are! Cook says you ain't got a penny to your name.

Crispian (*moving threatening up* R *of the table* LC) Look here—you clear out!

William (*moving to the door up* L) Bloomin' little toffs—I don't think. Dependants! Yah! (*He puts his tongue out*) Boo!

Crispian runs at William who exits hastily up L. *Rosamund eases* C

Crispian (*moving to* L *of the table* LC. *Sadly*) Dependants! There, you heard it. Even William calls us that.

Rosamund Yes, he's copying Uncle Joseph and Aunt Matilda—they're always calling us dependants.

Crispian (*perching himself on the downstage end of the table* LC) It was different when Uncle Matthew was alive.

Rosamund Dear Uncle Matthew—he was so good to us. I wonder what he'd say if he knew Uncle Joseph and Aunt Matilda had turned his lovely home into an hotel.

Crispian Yes, and if he could see how they treat us! If only father and mother were not dead!

Rosamund (*moving to* R *of Crispian and trying to find words to break her good news to him; eagerly*) Cris—perhaps they're not!

Crispian (*shaking his head*) No, there's no hope. It's six months now since their plane was lost and they've never been heard of since. And we were to have been together this Christmas. (*His voice breaks a little*) Oh, Mother!   2

Rosamund (*holding Crispian's right arm*) Cris, don't!

Crispian turns his back to Rosamund to hide his emotion

The voice of Vera Carey, the children's mother, is heard singing softly off stage during the following scene

Vera (*off*) "Rock-a-bye slumber comes soft from the West,
        Mother is calling her babes to the nest,
        Far-flying birdies sail home on tired wing,
        When all the world's mothers their cradle-song sing.
        Rock-a-bye sh-oo, Rock-a-bye sh-oo."

Crispian (*in a stifled voice*) It's worse for me. You saw her two years ago, but it's four years since I was in Hong Kong; and you don't know how I long to see her—if only to hear her say "Cris" once again. (*He pauses*) Do you remember that song she used to sing us when we were quite small?

Rosamund You mean the "Rock-a-bye Slumber" song?

Crispian Yes.

Rosamund Sometimes I seem to hear her singing it.

Crispian So do I. (*They stand as the song dies away—overcoming his emotion*) And to think we shall never see her again! (*He rises and moves to* L *of the table* LC)

Rosamund (*moving below the table* LC, *eagerly*) Cris! Cris! you may, if only you are brave enough.

Crispian (*turning sharply to face Rosamund, amazed*) Brave enough?

Rosamund Oh, I don't know how to tell you! You remember that wonderful book "The Land Where the Rainbow Ends" that Uncle Matthew used to read to us?

Crispian Yes?

Rosamund Well, this morning I suddenly thought of it, and I've been reading it. It's the most glorious, happiest land in all the world. And, oh

Cris, there's no time to tell you in bits—(*she moves to* R *of Crispian and puts her left hand on his right shoulder*) father and mother are there!

Crispian (*amazed*) Father and Mother?

Rosamund Yes. The book says, "All lost loved ones are found where the rainbow ends."

Crispian (*excitedly*) But how can we get there?

Rosamund The book tells us the way. It says there are dangers and perils on the journey, for you have to pass through the Dragon country. Now all we have to do is read the directions and leave this house as soon as possible.

Crispian Leave this house! If only we could!

Matilda (*off*) Crispian! Crispian!

Crispian Look out—Aunt Matilda!

Rosamund The book! (*Runs to the steps, picks up book*)

Crispian crosses to L *of Rosamund. Matilda Flint the children's aunt, enters up* L. *She is followed by William, who stand up* R *and rubs his arm. Matilda is an elderly plain woman, severe looking, thin and wiry. Her hair is grey but in the front she wears an almost jet-black toupee. She is dressed for the evening. She carries a large hand-bag and wears a coloured scarf over her shoulders*

Matilda (*as she enters*) Crispian, what is this I hear? (*she moves* C)

Cubs rises, moves to R *of Matilda and growls at her*

(*Shaking her fist at Cubs*) Lie down! (*To Crispian*) Stop that brute!

Crispian (*to Cubs*) Lie down, old chap.

Cubs growls under his breath and snuffles around Matilda's ankles. Rosamund crosses to R *of the table* LC

Matilda (*shooing Cubs up* RC) Horrid creature! (*To William*) Now, my boy, is it true that Crispian thrashed you?

William (*moving to* L *of Matilda*) Yes, ma'am. I'm all black and blue—I'll show you, ma'am.

Matilda (*with dignity*) Thank you, William, *no*! (*To Crispian*) So you actually dared to lay hands on William, did you?

Crispian (*defiantly*) Well, he shouldn't ill-treat Cubs. If he does, he shall pay for it.

Matilda So that's your tone, is it? (*To William*) You may go, my boy—and don't be afraid. If the brute growls at you again, he shall be poisoned.

Cubs, very startled, jumps in the air, then moves up C. *William grins*

Crispian }
Rosamund } (*together*) Poisoned!

Matilda (*Crosses towards table* LC) What's that on the floor?

William A packet of pins, ma'am. (*Picks them up*)

Matilda (*at table*) Labels!—and rope on the table—they must belong to

Monsieur Bertrand. (*To William*) Put them all on that packing-case, William—(*indicates packing-case up* RC) Then you can go.

William picks up labels and rope and puts them with the pins on the packing-case—as he crosses to door up L *he passes Cubs who growls at him— William makes a hasty exit as Crispian calls Cubs to him*

Matilda (*moving* C) What right have you to keep an animal at all, when you are utterly dependent on your uncle and myself for the very bread you eat? And I may as well tell you now that your Uncle has no intention of continuing your expensive educations. You will therefore neither of you be returning to your schools next term.

Crispian }
Rosamund } (*together*) Not returning to school?

Matilda Your Uncle is making other arrangements for your education until you are old enough to earn your own living. Crispian will then join his Uncle's firm as office boy.

Rosamund But Cris is to go to the University—father said so.

Matilda And I shall find plenty of work for *you* to do in the hotel. Which reminds me, we are short of staff so you can both make yourselves useful these holidays—you in the kitchen (*to Rosamund*) and you, Crispian can help with odd jobs—William will show you what to do.

Crispian *William!*

Matilda You will both of you report for duty before breakfast tomorrow.

Rosamund touches Crispian's left hand

Rosamund (*whispering to Crispian*) Tomorrow we shan't be here!

Crispian looks startled, then realizes what Rosamund means and clasps her hand

Matilda (*turning*) What are you whispering about? Leave this room—a library is no place for children.

Rosamund Dear Uncle Matthew loved us to be here.

Matilda Don't quote your Uncle Matthew to me. He hadn't an ounce of common sense for all his learning—squandering his money travelling to the most God-forsaken corners of the earth, buying any musty book or dirty rubbish that was offered him. (*She glances round room*) However, as this library will now be used for other purposes, it will all be sold and taken away tomorrow.

Rosamund }
Crispian } (*moving* C *together*) Sold!

Matilda (*moving down* R *maliciously*) Yes—*sold*! Monsieur Bertrand, the dealer, is here now and has already taken an inventory of every book in it.

Rosamund (*glancing fearfully at the book in her hand*) *Every* book?

Matilda Don't repeat my words, child. He is staying to dinner tonight in order to settle matters with your Uncle afterwards.

A murmur of voices is heard off L

Ah, here comes your uncle. Now be off to bed, both of you.

Cubs moves to L of Matilda

And you will neither of you have any supper for your insolence. (*Cubs growls at Matilda*) (*Very frightened*) And take that brute with you.

Cubs makes a dash at Matilda and worries her ankle as she exists hastily down R

Rosamund (*in a panic*) The book—the book—I *must* keep it!
Crispian You can't, they're coming. Hide—quick!

Rosamund runs to table LC and hides under it, the long table-cloth conceals her. Crispian moves to door up L followed by Cubs. As they do so Joseph Flint and Monsieur Bertrand enter up L. Joseph is a tall, thin man with arms that are too long for his coat-sleeves. He has a finicking, aggravating, mock-playful manner. Bertrand, a curio dealer, is dark and suave. He speaks English with a foreign accent. Joseph grabs Crispian by his left ear

Joseph (*leading Crispian to C*) What are you doing here? This is no fit place for a boy—an *office boy*. (*He sniggers*)

Bertrand eases down R of the table LC. Cubs moves to L of Joseph and growls at him. Joseph releases Crispian's ear.

(*turns, startled*) Ah, what have we here? The little lion-cub. You know, Bertrand, I'm very fond of animals—I can do anything with an animal—now just you watch me. (*He very bravely strolls to Cubs*) Nice pussy—puss puss!

Cubs growls furiously, and makes a dash at Joseph

Joseph (*dodging quickly behind Bertrand*) It's all right, Bertrand, don't be afraid. (*He gingerly pushes the reluctant Bertrand in front of him towards Cubs*) Lions belong to the cat-tribe, you know—we'll talk to him in his own language. Mee-ow! Me-ow!

Cubs resents this and makes a dash at the two men who retreat down L. They make another cautious advance. This time, Cubs dashes at Joseph and chases him up L of the table LC across to R and round the steps. Joseph, badly scared, climbs the steps and sits at the top. Cubs sits at the bottom of the steps, looks up at Joseph and growls

Joseph (*feels much safer and taunts Cubs*) Cross fingers! Can't touch me! (*Cubs growls and jumps up at Joseph's legs*) Doesn't like his Uncle Joseph, eh? Never mind—we'll have him skinned and made into a nice rug for the office. (*He laughs uproariously*) So much safer that way! (*Cubs growls more fiercely than ever*)
Crispian (*moving to the door up L unable to bear any more*) Oh, come on, Cubs.

He exits up L. *Cubs is about to follow when he sees Bertrand, moves quickly
to him and sniffs his ankles. Bertrand yells with fear. Joseph laughs so
heartily that he falls off the steps. Cubs exits up* L. *Bertrand crosses to* L
of Joseph and helps him to rise

Joseph Excuse me, my dear Bertrand, but whenever I see that boy, I must
laugh. Do you know, he ought to be master here. It was all the result of
poor dear Matthew scorning legal advice. So I, Joseph Flint, Solicitor, of
Bloomsbury, step into everything. (*In his excitement he steps on
Bertrand's foot*)

Bertrand reacts

Pardon, Bertrand, pardon! But now to business (*Glances round room*)
You have offered me a miserable sum, Bertrand—miserable. Poor dear
Matthew spent a fortune on these treasures.
Bertrand It is the best I can do.
Joseph Nonsense, nonsense! Two hundred pounds for all this! Absurd!
You must make it another two hundred.
Bertrand (*throwing up his arms in dismay*) Another two hundred pounds.
Ce n'est pas possible!
Joseph (*moving to Persian mat up* c) Temper, temper! Never show temper,
Bertrand. (*He lifts a corner of the mat and displays a label on the under-
side of it*) Now perhaps this will interest you.
Bertrand (*moving up* c) Ziz—what is ziz?
Joseph Persian—every inch.
Bertrand (*spurning the mat with his foot*) Rubbish! Not worth the taking
away. (*He crosses down* R)
Joseph Wait! Let me read you the legend attached to it. (*He kneels*) In
Matthew's own handwriting—most interesting. (*He reads the label*)
"Magic carpet."

Rosamund peeps out from under table and listens breathlessly

Bertrand (*moving up to Joseph*) Magic carpet?
Joseph "Bought of a Mersian Perchant . . ."
Bertrand You mean a Persian Merchant.
Joseph (*reading*) "Bought of a Persian Merchant, Mashad, January,
nineteen-forty." Listen!
    "If faith thou hast call loud and clear,
    'Oh, Carpet's Genie, now appear'
    At thy command thy slave he'll be,
    And carry thee o'er land and sea."
Wonderful! Beats any jet-plane hollow. Just believe, and there you are!
Why, Bertrand, one of your millionaire curio-collectors would jump at
it. (*He rises*)
Bertrand (*angrily*) Do you take me for a child to believe such foolishness?
You waste your time and mine, my friend. (*Moves down* c)
Joseph (*moving down* c) Ah, temper again! Now wait a minute—if you
won't buy the carpet, what about the books?

Bertrand (*moving to* R *of Joseph*) Ah, yes, ze books.

Joseph I'll tell you something. (*Very confidentially*) There is one book in this library that Matthew said he would not sell for it's weight in gold.

Bertrand (*interested*) So! What was the name of the book?

Joseph Now let me see. It was—it was . . .

Bertrand (*with inspiration*) Was it "Mrs. Beeton's Bookery Cook?"

Joseph No, no!

Bertrand "Little Rude Riding Head?"

Joseph No, no! Ah, I remember! "*Where the Rainbow Ends*".

Rosamund, in dismay, withdraws her head

Bertrand "Where the Rainbow Ends". Ah, I remember! (*He takes some lists from his pocket*) I have it in the inventory. (*He turns over pages*) Ah, here it is (*He reads*) "Where the Rainbow Ends" Shelf three, number one hundred and fifty." (*He moves to the bookshelves* R *and searches along shelf*) One hundred and forty-eight, one hundred and forty-nine— (*With concern*) one hundred and fifty-one . . . Mon Dieu! The book is gone!

Joseph Gone! Impossible! (*He moves up to book-shelves* L *of Bertrand*) Good heavens! It has.

Bertrand (*crossing to* R *of the table* LC) It was there this morning. I saw it. (*He replaces the inventory in his pocket*)

Joseph (*crossing to* R *of Bertrand; suspiciously*) Strange—no one has been in the library since *you* left it.

Bertrand No, no, you forget the boy, your nephew. It is he who has taken it. Send for him.

Joseph (*easing* C *watching Bertrand keenly*) Nonsense! He never reads a line if he can help it—likes toffee better than books. (*Moves to* R *of Bertrand. Knowingly*) No, no, my friend—you'll find the book—if you look in the—(*He taps Bertrand's pockets*) right place.

The sound of a gong is heard off R. *William enters down* R. *Bertrand looks on table* LC *for the book. Joseph turns to William.*

William (*announcing*) Dinner is served! (*He stands above door down* R)

Bertrand is just about to look under the table when Joseph turns to him

Joseph Now, my dear Bertrand—what are you doing?

Bertrand (*turning to Joseph*) Looking for the wonderful book.

Joseph (*leading Bertrand to* C) You're in a wretched buying mood this evening, Bertrand. But perhaps you'll be better after dinner. (*He signs for Bertrand to pass*) After you.

Bertrand No, no. (*With an elaborate bow*) After you.

Joseph No, no. You are my guest. (*He imitates Bertrand's bow*) You go first.

Bertrand (*crossing below Joseph to the door down* R) Oh, very well, if you insist. Toujours la politesse!

Joseph (*bowing*) La plume de ma tante! (*As Bertrand passes him he stealthily puts his hand in Bertrand's pocket*)
Bertrand (*stopping and turning*) Monsieur! What are you doing with my hand in your pocket?

Joseph apologises profusely in dumb show as he and Bertrand exit down R

William switches off the centre light and table lamp from the switches above **3** *the door down* R, *closes the door, then moves quietly to the windows up* C. *Rosamund, thinking the room is empty, comes out from her hiding-place and puts the book on the table* LC. *William sees her and hides quickly behind the curtain* R *of the windows. Rosamund runs to the mat up* C, *kneels, turns up the corner and reads the label*

Rosamund (*reading*) "If faith thou hast call loud and clear,
            'Oh, Carpet's Genie, now appear' "

A blue light floods the mat

(*she rises*) The Magic Carpet! (*She runs to the door up* L *and calls*) Crispian! Crispian, come here!

William peers out from behind the curtain

William Blimey! I must watch this! (*He withdraws his head*)

The blue light fades out. Crispian enters up L *and closes the door behind him*

Rosamund (*leading Crispian to mat*) Look, Crispian—(*she stands* R *of the mat*) The Magic Carpet!
Crispian (*standing* L *of the mat*) Nonsense! Why, it's only an old mat (*He spurns it with his foot*)
Rosamund (*kneeling and showing Crispian the label*) No, it isn't. It's the Magic Carpet! See what it says here.

Crispian kneels and reads the label

Crispian (*reading without conviction*)
            "If faith thou hast call loud and clear,
            'Oh, Carpet's Genie, now appear'
            At thy command thy slave he'll be,
            And carry thee o'er land and sea."
(*he rises*) What rot! (*He moves to* R *of the table* LC)
Rosamund (*rising and moving down* R) Oh, Cris, you're not going to be like the grown-up people and only believe what you see. Why, it glowed in the dark! (*She switches on the table-lamp from the switch above door down* R)
Crispian (*perching himself on the* R *edge of the table* LC) That's nothing, things do glow in the dark. Fish for instance, and the eyes of animals.
Rosamund (*moving* C) But *never* carpets! How tiresome you are. No one

ever had such a chance and you're going to spoil it all by not believing. Why, even the flowers know better than that.

Crispian Flowers?

Rosamund Yes. Think how dark to the snowdrop underground the earth must seem: but because she *believes* that above the hard blackness the sun is shining and the birds are singing, she goes on thrusting up and up, until one day she stands in the sunlight—the first darling flower of spring. That's the believing we want, Cris, or the carpet won't move.

Crispian (*doggedly*) How can it?

The sound of a clatter of plates is heard off R

Rosamund (*moving to R of Crispian: anxiously*) That's the meat going in. Do hurry up! You know Aunt Matilda's got her new teeth—and she always was a quick eater.

Crispian (*rising, desperately*) Well, if I *say* I believe?

Rosamund It's not the saying, it's the believing. Oh, think, Cris, what a **4** glorious adventure—(*she moves and stands R of the mat up C*)—and all you have to do is to stand so—(*she holds her arms out over the mat*)—and believe this *is* the Magic Carpet. Then you give the call, loud and clear—"Oh, Carpet's Genie, now appear".

A blue light floods the mat

(*in ecstasy*) Oh, Cris, look! It's beginning! It's true, it's true—the Genie is coming! Oh, quick—give the call loud and clear.

Crispian moves quickly to L of the mat and holds out his arms over it

Crispian "Oh, Carpet's Genie, now appear"!

The Genie rises slowly through the mat. He is a powerfully built man, oriental in appearance and dress, with ear-rings and anklets

Genie (*salaaming*) The Slave of the Carpet awaits your command.

Crispian (*to Rosamund*) W-what shall I say to him?

Rosamund (*easing RC*) I know. (*She turns to the Genie. Very grandly*) Attend to me, then, and if you are able—convey us presently to where the rainbow ends.

The Genie salaams

Genie (*salaaming*) Your commands shall be obeyed. Be it known to you that to all who have sufficient faith to summon me, are granted two wishes, which must be fulfilled before we start our journey. Therefore, deliberate and decide, for time is short and we have far to travel.

Crispian Two wishes each! What on earth shall I wish for?

A bell is heard to ring off R. Rosamund runs quickly to the door down R, listens a moment, then runs to R of the Genie

Rosamund (*clapping her hands, hastily*) I wish that those three in the dining-room shall begin their dinner all over again.

The Genie salaams, then points to the door down R

Crispian (*in disgust*) I say, what a rotten wish!
Rosamund No it wasn't. The bell rang for coffee. In another five minutes
they would all have been in here. (*She runs to the door down* R)

Crispian crosses to L *of Rosamund. She opens the door down* R *and looks off*

And now (*she gurgles with delight*) come and see.

She pulls Crispian to the door. The sound of a clatter of plates is heard off R

Crispian (*looking off down* R) They're taking in the soup again! (*He laughs*)
Rosamund (*laughing*) Yes. Isn't it splendid? (*She closes the door*)
Crispian Won't they all get jolly indigestion!

Cub's whimper is heard off up L

Rosamund What's that?
Crispian (*crossing to the door up* L) It's Cubs.
Rosamund (*moving* RC) Of course we couldn't leave him, the pet.
Crispian (*opening the door up* L) Of course not.

Cubs enters friskily up L. *He crosses below Crispian to* L *of the Genie—
starts, is momentarily doubtful, sniffs at the Genie's legs and is satisfied he is
a friend*

Crispian (*closes the door. To Cubs*) Lie down by the fire, old chap.

*Cubs crosses to the fireplace, warms his front paws, then curls up on the
hearth-rug*

Rosamund Oh, Cris, do hurry up with your wishes, or we shall have to
send in dinner again—and that would be a waste.
Crispian (*easing above the table* LC) At any rate, we'd get one back on the
cook!
Rosamund Oh, *do* hurry up!
Crispian (*crossing to* L *of Rosamund*) Well, it seems to me that this is going
to be a man's job—and there ought to be two of us—and I know Blunders
would just jump at it.
Rosamund Blunders?
Crispian Yes. Jim Blunders. He's our Rugger Captain—a grand bloke,
and just the sort to help us. (*He moves to the* R *of Genie*) I shall wish for
him. (*He raises his hands to clap them*)
Rosamund (*quickly*) Be careful! Remember, a person who couldn't believe
would prevent our starting. (*She moves down* RC)
Crispian Oh, Jim's all right! (*He claps his hands. To the Genie*) I wish for
Jim Blunders—(*he glances at Rosamund's back*) and his sister too. (*He
eases* RC)

The Genie salaams and points to the door up L. *Jim and Betty Blunders enter
up* L *as if they had been blown on. They both look around the room in great*

*astonishment. Jim is a slightly bigger boy than Crispian. He wears a
similar blazer. Betty is a charming little girl aged about ten*

Crispian By Jove! That was quick!
Jim (*crossing to Crispian, joyfully*) Hallo, Cris!
Crispian Hallo, old chap (*He shakes hands with Jim*)
Rosamund (*astounded*) Why, there are two of them!
Crispian (*introducing*) Jim Blunders—my sister Rosamund.

*Jim bows. Rosamund returns the bow with dignity. Betty eases shyly to R of
the table* LC

Rosamund (*looking from Jim to Betty*) But I don't understand. (*To Betty*)
Who are you? And where did you come from?

Betty looks shyly at the floor

Crispian (*a bit embarrassed*) Oh it's all right (*He introduces*) Miss Betty
Blunders—my sister, Rosamund.
Rosamund (*after a pause*) I still don't understand—(*to Betty, rather coldly*)
Cris wished for your brother . . .
Crispian (*moving to Rosamund*) Oh, hang it all, Rosamund, if you must
know—I said to the Genie "and Blunder's sister too".
Rosamund (*crossing to Betty*) Of course if that's the case, (*Very affably*) I'm
very glad to meet you.

The girls hug each other

Jim (*indicating the Genie*) Hullo! What's that?
Crispian Oh, a friend of ours—the Genie.
Jim (*bowing to the Genie*) How do you do?

The Genie salaams

Rosamund Well, that's your two wishes gone, anyhow, and now—(*she
crosses thoughtfully below the table* LC)—for mine. (*She sits on down-stage
edge of the table and faces the audience*)
Jim I say, Cris, what's up?
Crispian Are you game for an adventure?
Jim Rather!
Crispian And you, Betty?

Betty nods

Jim (*easing down* C) Oh, she's keen enough. What adventure?

There is a pause as Crispian moves to the door down R *and listens for a
moment*

Crispian (*moving to* R *of Jim*) We are going to find our father and mother.
We believe they are in the land where the rainbow ends. Will you and
Betty come with us?
Jim Rather!
Crispian (*crossing below Jim to* R *of Betty*) And you, Betty? (*Betty nods. He*

turns to Jim) I must tell you that there is danger in it. We have to pass through the Dragon country.

Jim Oh, a dragon or two won't matter, will it, Betty?

Betty Well—not *more* than two.

Rosamund (*who has been immersed in thought—suddenly and excitedly*) Oh, it's splendid! You'll never guess—it's too lovely!

They all gather round Rosamund. Betty moves to R of her. Crispian moves to R of Betty. Jim runs above the table LC and down L of Rosamund. Cubs wakes up and sits listening with his head on one side

All (*ad lib*) What is it? What is it? Hurry up, get on!

Rosamund Now you know we are starting on a journey of perils and dangers. Oh, it's too lovely! . . . Well, I'm going to wish for a knight to fight for us—

All (*ad lib, excitedly*) A knight!

Rosamund As they did in the olden days. (*She jumps off the table*) And who do you think he is? The knight who fought the Dragon before—St George of England! (*She runs to L of the Genie*)

All (*ad lib. Very thrilled*) St George! St George!

Rosamund claps her hands twice without speaking

Rosamund (*very imperiously*) St George! Let him appear!

The Genie salaams and points to the door down R which slowly opens. St George enters and stands in the shadows just above the door. He is handsome, golden-haired and soldierly looking. He is clad in a long grey cloak. The children are astounded and puzzled at his appearance

Rosamund (*moves c. To St George, shyly*) I beg your pardon—but I fear there's been some mistake. (*She turns to Genie*) Genie, you've sent us the wrong man. I wished for St George.

St George (*bowing with courtly grace*) Lady, I am he.

The children stare in amazement

Rosamund (*politely but incredulously*) You—you—St George?

Cubs shakes his head

Oh, I beg your pardon. I'm so sorry. I didn't recognize you dressed like that.

St George Thus humbly clad, un-noted and unsung, do I lie hidden in the hearts of men.

Rosamund (*dismayed*) But you have no armour—no sword.

St George None that the eye can see. Yet at duty's call, quick as in days of old, shall this same sword leap from it's scabbard to defend the right. (*He turns slightly as if to exit*)

Rosamund Oh, please don't go. You (*hesitantly*) are my wish, you know.

St George What would you, lady?

Rosamund (*very nervously*) Oh, I hope you'll excuse me, but you see—

having read in several books of your chivalry to maidens in distress, and the splendid way you have of killing dragons—I ventured to think—to hope—you'd be our knight and fight for us. (*She pauses*)

St George looks steadily at Rosamund

Perhaps I shouldn't have troubled you at such a time—but I am a maiden in danger, and I ask your aid.   5

There is a blinding flash, during which St George's cloak vanishes—snatched from him through the gap in the scenery above door down R. St George is now revealed in dazzling armour, with his sword at his side, and his cloak with a red cross on his shoulders

All (*ad lib; in ecstasy*) St George! St George!

Cubs run down LC and waves his arms frantically

St George moves down RC

Rosamund (*standing a little up L of St George; tremulously*) Oh, oh, you are —really simply *splendid*! I hope you won't think this adventure too beneath you. I know we don't appear much in distress as you see us at present—but there are Uncle Joseph and Aunt Matilda in the next room—who hate us—and a real dragon to fight a little further on. Oh, and remembering the kind interest you take in distressed maidens—(*hesitantly*)—perhaps you will be glad to hear there is another one here besides myself. (*She crosses to Betty, takes her by the hand, and leads her LC and introduces her*). Miss Betty Blunders, distressed maiden—St George.

Betty moves C very timidly, curtsies three times to St George, then turns and crosses hurriedly to L of Jim. St George bows gallantly to Betty

(*She continues the introductions*) Mr Jim Blunders . . .

Jim bows

My brother, Crispian Carey.

Crispian crosses to L of St George and bows

St George Crispian! That's a good name. We did some fine work once on Crispian's Day.
Crispian Rather—Agincourt! But were you there, sir? They never mentioned it.
St George No. You see it was my chum Crispian's turn. But I was there sure enough—a Patron Saint could hardly miss a chance like that.
Rosamund Oh, please do tell us all about it.
All (*ad lib*) Please do!

Cubs whines his "please do"

Rosamund eases above the table LC

Crispian stands RC

St George (*moving a little up* C *and turning*) Well, you know how few there were of us—and how through the rain-swept night had risen like fateful menace those bold songs of France. E'er morning dawned, I summoned by the King, stood there within his tent. Invisible to all others, he saw and hailed me, calling me—brother, comrade—England. At his side that morn did I ride forth; then sighting the foe, at his desire, his unseen aide-de-camp, did I ride from rank to rank. Did some poor country lad sicken at sight of blood, I bade the man in him awake for England's sake. Where grim and swift, mid shriek of arrows sped the mighty archers sweated at their toil, I whispered to each stout heart the message of their King; thus one and all, catching his spirit like lions did they fight, crying amidst the din and toil of battle (*he draws his sword*) "God for Harry—England and St George".

All (*ad lib; excitedly*) St George! St George!

Betty runs to St George and faces him

Betty (*excitedly*) St George! St George!

St George smiles and sheathes his sword

Betty, suddenly abashed by her own temerity, runs L *to Jim, who puts his arm round her*

St George But times are changed—I and my brother saints are now allied with all men and goodwill throughout the world to fight the Dragon King, the mortal enemy of all who hope for peace and brotherhood. 'Tis he who sows mistrust and discord in men's hearts, and thus by setting one against the other, he reaps the harvest of their discontent. Beneath his sway violence, corruption, tyranny and hate ravage the earth, with terror at their heels, while law and order crumble in their wake—and from the chaos of a shattered world he schemes to snatch his final victory —to gain dominion over all mankind, and hold them ever subject to his will . . . (*He turns* C) Men of goodwill, of every race and creed—'tis your disunity that is his strength—if you will but forget your differences and pledge yourselves unto this common cause, to overcome the evils of the world, united you can break the Dragon's power and build, through Peace, a better world for all! (*He moves down* RC) Now must I go . . .

Rosamund (*moving to* L *of St George*) Oh, no!

St George But only from your sight. (*He holds his left hand out over Rosamund's head*) Dear maid, remember though you see me not—that I am ever with you—your faithful guardian knight. No foe of yours that is not a foe of mine. No dangers yours that are not shared by me. No wrong of yours that I will not redress. (*He draws his sword and kneels*) Here do I swear myself once more unto this cause. (*He kisses the hilt of his sword*) God for Freedom, Justice and the Right!

The lights black-out

St George rises and exits, unseen, down R

When the lights come up again, the children look around the room, astonished.

Cubs moves to the fireplace and looks up the chimney

Rosamund Isn't he a darling?

Betty crosses to L *of Rosamund*

Crispian (*easing down* LC) Splendid!
Jim Smashing!
Betty Lovely!

Cubs jumps up and down and nods his head in agreement

A bell is heard to ring off R

Rosamund (*runs to the door down* R, *opens it and looks off*) That's the coffee going in again. (*She closes the door*) Oh, do hurry up, or they'll catch us!

Crispian moves to R *of the Genie and claps his hands*

Crispian (*to the Genie*) We wish to go at once to where the rainbow ends. **7**
Genie (*salaaming*) It shall be as you desire. Yet—beware—beware! Guard the carpet well. If but it's edge, or one shred be torn from it and fall into the hands of those who wish you ill, they can at once summon the enemy, the mighty Dragon King, who will pursue and perchance overtake us. (*He steps off the mat and stands above it*) Therefore—beware—and guard the carpet well!
Crispian Phew! If Uncle Joseph could get a bit!
Rosamund (*crossing quickly above the table* LC) Oh, do be quick! (*Picks up the book from the table*) We must be labelled! (*She runs across to the packing case up* L, *kneels down and hastily scribbles on one of the labels there*)
Crispian Cubby's Mixture, we mustn't forget that! (*Picks up Mixture from table up* R. *To Cubs*) Come along, Cubs. (*Cubs runs to mat and sits on it*) You hang on to it. (*Gives Cubs bottle which he hugs to him*)
Jim (*who has followed Rosamund to packing-case*) Let me tie that label on for you. (*Takes label from Rosamund and ties it to a corner of the mat*)
Crispian Come along. Betty! (*Takes her hand and leads her up to mat*) Do hurry up, Rosamund!
Rosamund One moment, these pins—they may be useful. (*She picks up packet of pins from packing-case and puts them in her pocket, then runs to mat*)
Crispian You girls in the middle . . . O.K. Blunders?

Jim steps on to mat. The girls crouch in the middle

Genie Are all prepared?
All (*together*) Yes!
Genie (*raising his arms*) Then *hold tight*!

As he does so William comes out from the curtain and unseen by the others tears off the label and with it a small piece of the carpet, and waves it above his head as the lights black-out

*During the black-out, the Genie, Cubs, Crispian, Rosamund, Jim and Betty
exit quickly by the french windows, taking the mat with them. William
stumbles to the door down* R *switches on the centre light and rushes off down* R

William (*shouting*) Mr Flint! Miss Flint! The children are flying away on a
carpet!

Exits

Crispian (*off up* C) By Jove! Look, Jim!
Rosamund (*off up* C) Betty, see, the stars!

*The carpet is seen to fly across outside the window. Matilda enters
hurriedly down* R. *She carries her bag and scarf*

Matilda (*as she enters, wildly*) The children! (*She crosses to the french
windows and looks off shrieking and gesticulating*)

Bertrand enters down R

Bertrand (*rushing to the french windows and calling*) Come back, come
back! The carpet—I must buy it!

Joseph enters excitedly down R. *He wears a top-hat and carries a whip.
Matilda turns and moves to* R *of the table* LC

Joseph (*as he enters*) What's this, what's this? (*He crosses to* L *of Bertrand
and looks off*) The carpet—the magic carpet! (*He calls*) Come back!
Come back!

William rushes on down R. *He holds the piece of carpet with label*

William (*running to Bertrand and waving the piece of carpet at him,
excitedly*) 'Ere, 'ere! I tore this off as they started flying. Rub it and you
can fetch 'em back.
Bertrand (*impatiently*) Out of ze way! (*Flings William off and rushes up to
window*)
William (*bumping into Matilda*) 'Ere, 'ere! Catch 'old of this and summon
the Dragon.
Matilda (*indignantly*) Take a month's notice! (*She pushes William to* C)

William staggers on to Joseph

William (*bumping into Joseph*) 'Ere, 'ere! See what's wrote on this!
Joseph (*gripping William by the arm and leading him down* C) What's wrote
on what? (*He takes the piece of carpet from William and reads the label*)
"To Where the Rainbow Ends."
William (*excitedly*) Yes—that's where they've gone—to find their father
and mother.
Joseph Their father and mother alive!
Matilda Alive! (*She crosses above Joseph and stands down* R)

Joseph Then I lose everything!

William No! No! This 'ere is magic.

Joseph ⎫
Matilda ⎭ (*together*) Magic!

William Yes. If you rub it, you can make the Dragon King fetch 'em back. (*He crosses and stands below the table* LC)

Bertrand (*looking off up* C) Mon Dieu! Mon Dieu! How fast ze carpet flies! They do escape! (*He turns and moves* LC)

Joseph (*moving to* L *of Matilda*) Escape—never! (*He rubs the piece of carpet*) Never—never—never!

There is a peal of thunder. The floor opens and the Dragon King appears **8**
from below in a cloud of smoke and a red glow. He is a tall majestic-looking man with a malevolent face. He is dressed in green scales and wears a dragon head-dress

Matilda (*shrieking*) Antedeluvian!

Bertrand It is ze devil! (*Flies off through french windows in terror*)

William hides under table LC

Joseph The Loch Ness Monster!

Dragon King (*very sternly*) Why have you summoned me? (*He sees the piece of carpet in Joseph's hand—with a cry of rage*) Ah, the Genie's carpet—'tis he, the friend of little children whom I hate! What want you with me?

Joseph Overtake the children and bring them back. (*He waves the piece of carpet*) This is the bond.

Dragon King (*proudly*) I need no bond. This Genie with his carpet doth ever from my power free those I would destroy. Revenge! Revenge! Come, let us be gone!

Joseph (*turning to Matilda and taking her arm*) Come on, Matilda!

Matilda (*holding back*) But—I can't go without a tooth brush.

Joseph (*grimly*) It's this—or we lose everything!

Dragon King (*turning and moving up* C) Let us be gone!

William creeps out of his hiding-place

Joseph Come along, Matilda! (*Drags her up* C. *Seizing the rope from packing-case up* RC)

Dragon King (*turning and raising his arms*) Are all prepared?

Matilda (*in consternation*) But I—I can't fly at my time of life!

Dragon King (*sardonically*) Calm yourself, madam, I always travel underground.

There is a peal of thunder. The party descend through the floor. A cloud of **9**
smoke is seen and a red glow. Matilda is heard to shriek as the CURTAIN *falls.*

   The CURTAIN *rises again and William is seen above the trap, gazing down and laughing, while Bertrand peeps fearfully through window up* C

CURTAIN

ACT II

The outskirts of the Dragon Wood. Late afternoon.

The R and L side of the scene have different aspects. The R side represents St George's territory and the L the Dragon King's country, and there is a distinct contrast between the light green ground R and the dark wood L. The R side of the woodland backcloth represents a sunny glade, there is a large grassy mound R that slopes towards C. The wings are of pretty woodland and rose trees. The flag of St George a red cross on a white ground, flies from a flag-staff above the mound. The L side of the backcloth is of dark rocks and dark woodland, and there are dark wood wings L. The flag of the Dragon King, a gold dragon on a green ground, flies from a flagstaff L at entrance to wood. If possible electric fans should be mounted behind the wings R and L to keep the flags fluttering

A large mushroom the height of a seat stands C

When the CURTAIN rises the sun is near setting, and the lights very gradually dim throughout the Act as it does so. The Magic Carpet is resting on the mound R and on it Betty, Jim and Rosamund are asleep. The book is on the mat beside Rosamund. Crispian sits on the mat. He has just woken up. Cubs is curled up asleep on the L end of the mat. His bottle of Mixture is beside him. They are on the piece of ground, which although it is in the heart of the Dragon King's country, belongs to St George: it is the place where he fought and overcame the Dragon long ago. On this spot the children are safe. The flags flutter in the light breeze. The Genie stands C his arms folded

Genie (*salaaming*) Behold, it is as you desire. (*He moves and stands up LC*)
Crispian (*rubbing his eyes*) We're not there already, are we? (*He looks round*) By Jove! What a wonderful place! (*He rises*) Rosamund—Blunders—wake up. We're there!
Rosamund (*rubbing her eyes and looking round*) So we are. How exciting! Why, we must have fallen asleep. (*She shakes Betty*) Betty, Betty, wake up. (*She stands up and jumps off the mound to C*)

Betty sits up sleepily, looks round, then stands up, jumps off the mound and eases up RC

Crispian (*kicking Jim*) Blunders, do wake up! (*He jumps off the mound and stands down R*)

Jim and Cubs roll off the mound

Jim (*sitting on the ground below mound, very sleepily*) Oh, do dry up! (*He yawns, then realizing where he is, jumps up and looks around*) I say, what a smashing place!

Cubs wakes up, looks around, then moves to Rosamund

Rosamund Come along, Cubs, you must be thirsty. (*She moves to the mound, picks up the bottle of Mixture, gives some to Cubs who drinks it with delight. Rosamund replaces the bottle on the mound*)
Crispian (*moving to flagstaff* R) I say, look at this flag!

They all group around the flagstaff R

Rosamund The Cross of St George! How splendid!
Crispian The Cross of St George!
Jim So it is!
Cubs Woof!
Rosamund (*indicating flag* L *fearfully*) Do you see this flag here?
Crispian (*turning and moving to* R *of Rosamund*) It has a dragon on it.
Jim (*moving* RC) So it has . . .

The sound of a low, deep rumble is heard off L. *They all run together in a group up* RC *and look off* L *in awe*

Crispian What was that?
Rosamund (*moving down* RC) You remember the Genie discovered that a piece of the carpet was missing soon after we started?
All (*with dismay*) Yes. (*They move down and cluster around Rosamund*)
Rosamund Suppose Uncle Joseph has found it!
All (*dismayed*) Oh!
Jim (*moving down* R *reassuringly*) Well, it's no use meeting trouble half-way—and as for that noise, this is probably a volcanic country.
Crispian Let's ask the Genie where we are. (*He moves* C, *faces the Genie and claps his hands*) We wish to know—where we are.   **11**
Genie (*salaaming*) Over sea, over land, mountains and plains, I, the Slave of the Carpet, have brought you hither. The evening star was your lamp, soft zephyrs your wings, the fleecy clouds your coverings. The spirits of the moon did bring you sleep—and while you slept came one in splendid armour——

The children look at one another

—riding a steed that faster than the scurrying clouds flew ever at your side in grand protection.
All (*ad lib, joyfully*) St George! St George!
Genie He did counsel me to bring you hither—for on this spot did this same knight, many hundred years ago, fight and o'ercome the mighty Dragon King—and in this, the very heart and fastness of the enemy's country (*He indicates the flag* R) set up his banner, beneath the shelter of which no ill can befall you. (*He points* R) Behold the light green ground of safety—(*he points* L) the dark of danger. There lies your path to where the rainbow ends. (*He crosses and goes up on to the mound*) Now must the book you carry be your guide, and faith and hope your helpers. I can do no more. (*He rolls up the Magic Carpet and puts it over his shoulder*) Farewell!

He flies across off L. *The children and Cubs group* L *of the mound and look* **12**
off L *following his unseen flight and from* L *round to* R

All (*ad lib*) Look! Look! There he goes. Look! Behind that cloud. How
fast he flies. Look! Look!

Will-o'-the-Wisp enters L. *He is a beautiful little creature, his head covered
with short flaxen curls, and is dressed in grey gossamer. He carries a reed
pipe. When he sees the children he hides behind a tree up* L. *A white spot-
light follows him wherever he goes*

Rosamund (*looking off* R) Dear old Genie. It's sad to lose him. (*She turns
and points off* L) Look, Betty, there lies our path to where the rainbow
ends, where we are going to find dear father and mother. Oh, mother,
mother, how we want you!

Cubs moves R

Betty Dear Rosamund, I hope you find her soon.   **13**

*Will comes out from behind tree. Cubs catches sight of him. Will dances first
one side of tree, then the other—Cubs does similar movements up and down* RC

Jim (*seeing Will*) Crispian! Crispian! Look! A Will-o'-the-Wisp!
Crispian By Jove, yes! Look, Rosamund!
Rosamund Look, Betty.
Jim Let's catch him.
Crispian Yes.

Jim and Crispian move down C *and endeavour to catch Will, who dances near
them mockingly and dodges around them*

Will   Yes, catch me do.
                                  I'm here, I'm there,
                                  I'm everywhere.
                                  Cuckoo! Cuckoo!

*He dodges between Jim and Crispian, who only succeed in catching each
other as he dances off* L. *Cubs sits on ground* C

Crispian (*moving down* LC) What a funny little chap!
Betty (*running to* L *and looking off*) He's gone into the wood!
Crispian (*moving quickly to* R *of Betty and taking hold of her arm*) Be careful,
Betty! Remember what the Genie said—don't leave St George's ground.

Betty shrugs her shoulders and looks longingly off L

Rosamund (*moving to the mound*) I must get the book and see what it says.
(*She sits on the mound, picks up the book, opens it and starts to read*)
Crispian (*moving* RC) And to think it was here they fought. I should like to
have seen them at it.
Jim So would I! (*Moves to* R *of Crispian*)

Some Rabbits creep out of wood cautiously L *and peep and play around the wings*

Betty (*enchanted*) Oh, do come and look at these rabbits. Such darlings! (*Pleadingly*) Oh, can't we go in?
Rosamund (*looking up from the book*) No, no, it's Dragon country. We must wait till sunrise.
Crispian (*disconcerted*) Why?
Jim Why sunrise?
Rosamund Because the book says the wood is full of dangers after sunset.
Crispian (*moving below the mound*) But that means we shall have to spend the night here.
Betty (*stamping her foot*) I *won't* spend the night here—it's horrid! (*She stamps down* C)
Jim (*moving to* R *of Betty, reprovingly*) Betty! That's a nice thing to say when you're out visiting.

Betty flounces L *and lies on the ground, facing wood. Cubs moves and lies beside her*

Rosamund I'm awfully sorry, Betty dear; but that's what the book says.
Crispian (*taking the book from Rosamund*) Here, Rosamund, let me see. (*He sits on the mound to* R *of Rosamund*)

Jim moves to the mound and sits L *of Rosamund. Betty and Cubs try to entice Rabbits out of wood*

Crispian (*reading*) "Now the Dragon's Wood lies but a day's travel from where the rainbow ends; and from here onward must all pilgrims go with none to aid them, save their own faith and courage. And let all enter the wood at sunrise, for when the sun sets the Dragon's power is at it's mightiest; the fearsome creatures of the night stalk through the forest, and tenfold are the devices and temptations laid to entrap the travellers."

Betty bursts out laughing at the antics of the Rabbits

Jim Betty, be quiet, and listen!

Betty, reproved, sits up very demurely with downcast eyes. Cubs follows and sits L *of mount*

Crispian (*reading*) "And let the travellers see that they cross the lake at the end of the wood only by the ford where grows the yellow mustard seed, for many essay a false crossing and perish in the waters."

Betty, her attention again distracted by Cub's antics with the Rabbits, **14** *giggles. A deep rumble is heard off* L. *The Rabbits exit in panic. Betty and Cubs run* L. *The other children all rise, very scared, and group* L *of mount*

Crispian What's that?

Rumble is heard again

Jim Hide! Quick!

Rosamund and Betty clasps hands and start to run L

Crispian No, No! Not that way—(*he points off down* R) This way!

He and Blunders catch hold of the girls and they all exit hurriedly, with Cubs, down R. *Dunks, the Dragon King's Chief Minister enters up* L *from wood, and crosses to* L *of the mound. He is older than the Dragon King and has grey-blue scales and a worm-like head-dress. His manner is servile and crafty. The sound of the rumble is heard off* L. *Dunks moves* C *and faces* L. *The Dragon King enters up* L. *Dunks salutes him with a low bow. The Dragon King barely returning his salute, strides down* LC *in a towering rage*

Dragon King Insufferable! Insufferable!

Dunks Your Majesty appears perturbed.

Dragon King (*crossing to* R) 'Tis so. He who this time doth hold the carpet of the Genie is a low, contemptible tyrant who, taking advantage of the power he holds, dares to trifle with *me*—a King!

Dunks Your Majesty forgets, 'tis but that you may wreak your vengeance on those whom the Carpet carries, that you deign to obey its summons.

Dragon King (*moving up* R *with a low hiss of contempt*) You watched here as I did command?

Dunks Yes, your Majesty. These children have already arrived.

Dragon King (*moving to* R *of Dunks*) Not one of them must leave my land alive! (*He takes Dunks by the arm and leads him down* L. *Confidentially*) Listen! These children have, to shield them from my wrath, invoked the aid of my most mortal foe, St George!

Dunks (*aghast*) St George!

Dragon King (*between his teeth*) Yes, he whose spirit it has been my plan to deaden in the hearts of every man. That spirit that forever foils my aim to hold dominion o'er the souls of men. (*He moves down* C) How often have I thought the battle won, when from the embers of the holocaust a single spark has kindled to a flame, and those I deemed subjected to my will have risen from the ashes of despair to light the torch of freedom once again. (*He gnashes his teeth and crosses to* R) To what heights has this spirit not led men in the past—to what greater heights may he not lead them in the future?

Dunks (*moving* C. *With meaning*) The future—your Majesty forgets the future is in *your* power.

Dragon King What mean you?

Dunks (*hissing*) The children!

Dragon King (*with a cry of triumph*) Ah! The children! (*He gloats*) Yes! The children shall be mine! Where are they now?

Dunks (*pointing off down* R) In yonder copse, your Majesty.

Dragon King (*strides* R *then pulling up suddenly; furious, indicating flag* R) Beneath that flag, where I am powerless! In the very heart of my kingdom, it thus mocks my power! (*He comes* C *and beckons to Dunks*)

Dunks crosses to L *of Dragon King*

Dragon King (*confidentially*) They must be decoyed from thence. Once in
the wood at nightfall where none can help them, my beasts of prey shall
hunt them down, till worn with hunger and fatigue, they shall be tempted
to eat of my dragon fruit, which robs men of their birthright of free-will
and holds them ever slaves of mine. (*He snorts*) See that a party of my
daintiest elves be here at sunset to—lure—them in.

Dunks Your Majesty shall be obeyed.

Dragon King As for this lawyer-uncle—his punishment I have planned. You
know the parents of these children were wrecked upon my coast. I will
contrive this very night that they are rescued—thus shall this lawyer lose
the estate he now falsely holds—and the children ne'er behold the parents
they come to find! Well, what think you?

Dunks (*moving* C) It is a right princely scheme, your Majesty. (*He bows*)

Dragon King (*moving* R) Where are the parents now?

Dunks Castaways on the Witch's Cove, sire.

Dragon King Enough. (*He raises his right arm*) Ye Spirits of the Air that **15**
me obey, ye Storm and Tempest Fiends—summon the Sea Witch to
me!

A peal of thunder is heard. The Sea Witch flies on L *on her broomstick. She
is old and hideous with lank white hair. She is dressed in cobweb grey*

Witch Master! Master! (*She crosses to* L *of Dragon King and cringes to
him*) What want you of me?

Dragon King (*towering over the Witch*) Listen and obey on pain of torture
that shall wrack thee with torment most horrible.

Witch (*cowering*) Nay, nay! Master, I obey.

Dragon King Search the seas for ship to England bound, and ere the sun
shall set, brew such a storm as shall drive it from its course to sight the
castaways on yonder coast.

Witch Too hard! Too hard! I'm old and scant of breath.

Dragon King Begone—or suffer what I did predict.

Witch Mercy! Mercy!

Dragon King Begone!

Witch   It shall be done
                            Ere set of sun.

Dragon King (*raising his arm*) Begone!

With a hideous screech of laughter the Witch flies off L

Dragon King (*with uplifted arms*) Revenge, revenge is mine!

The sound of groaning and moaning is heard off up L. *Dunks moves up* C *and
looks off* L

Dunks These people do approach, your Majesty.

Dragon King (*crossing to* L) Receive them.

He exits L. *Dunks moves and stands* C *above the mound. Joseph and Matilda enter up* L. *Matilda is in a half-fainting condition, her eyes are closed and Joseph supports her. She looks dishevelled and her toupee is askew. She wears her scarf over her shoulders and carries her bag. Joseph also looks rather dishevelled. He wears his top-hat and carries his whip*

Joseph (*half leading, half dragging Matilda* C) Come along, Matilda! Don't be foolish! We have arrived in the Dragon's country.

Matilda opens her eyes, gives one look, utters a piercing shriek and collapses against Joseph

Joseph (*depositing her upon the mushroom* C *with little ceremony. Seizes her right hand and slaps it spitefully*) Don't give way, Matilda—for heaven's sake control yourself.
Matilda (*with a groan*) Oh, oh, where am I? Tell me, am I still Miss Matilda Flint?
Joseph (*snappishly*) Yes, yes, you're still *Miss* Matilda Flint and likely to remain *Miss* Flint for ever.

Matilda gives a protesting shriek and closes her eyes and collapses again

Joseph (*unfeelingly*) *Do* pull yourself together!
Matilda (*faintly*) But how did I come here? Was it a coal-mine? Will someone explain?

Dunks moves slowly and softly to R *of Joseph. Neither Matilda nor Joseph notice him*

Joseph What does it matter whether you understand or not? One more ignorant woman in the world won't be noticed. What *does* matter is— (*he looks around*)—where are the children? (*He sees Dunks. He does a double take and his eyes open with terror. After a moment he pulls himself together, chuckles with malicious glee and turns to Matilda, who is rocking herself to and fro*) Matilda! Matilda!

Matilda takes no notice. He prods her with his whip

Do pull yourself together, Matilda—and—(*softly*)—put your toupee straight.
Matilda (*opening her eyes, disconcerted*) What's the matter with my toupee? (*She tries to straighten it*)

Dunks folds his arms and looks on

Joseph (*with a glance over his right shoulder at Dunks*) There is a—gentle-man—to see you. (*He laughs at his own joke*)
Matilda Oh, a gentleman to see me! (*She rises, very fussed and tidies herself*)

Joseph steps back a pace

I do hope I look nice . . . (*She turns, sees Dunks and screams with terror*) Oh, Oh, what is it?

Joseph (*laughing at Matilda's consternation*) Well, perhaps I should have said there was a prehistoric male creature present. Allow me to introduce you—(*he indicates Dunks*)—Prehistoric—(*he indicates Matilda*)—Antique! Now you know each other. (*He moves up* C *to* L)

Matilda turns nervously to Dunks and goes to shake hands with him. Dunks raises his arms and performs a bow so grotesquely that Matilda screams with fright and flies to Joseph, who is laughing and thoroughly enjoying her discomfiture

Matilda Oh! I thought he was going to bite me!

Joseph seats her on mushroom

   Dunks eases to L *of mound*

Joseph (*crossing to* L *of Dunks*) Where is His Majesty the Dragon King? I do not see him.

Dunks His Majesty is slightly fatigued. I must beg you to excuse him.

Joseph (*taking the piece of carpet from his pocket*) His Majesty seems to forget that at present he is very much—er—on the *tapis*! (*He flourishes the piece of carpet in Dunk's face*)

Dunks, furious, tries to snatch the piece of carpet

(*He laughs and holds the piece of carpet behind his back*) His Majesty also seems to have overlooked that he undertook to overtake the children. (*He waves the piece of carpet again*) I must ask His Majesty to deliver them to me at once.

Dunks (*in suppressed wrath*) 'Tis useless! The children have placed themselves outside His Majesty's territory—there—(*he indicates the flag* R)—under the protection of *that flag*.

He makes a furious gesture at the flag and crosses and exits angrily L

Joseph looks after him in surprise, then looks at the flag R *and bursts into derisive laughter*

Joseph (*pointing to flag* R) That! Surely His Majesty can't be afraid of *that*! Why it's only a little bit of bunting! (*Laughs sneeringly*)

Matilda Ridiculous!

Joseph And to think the children believe they are safe under its power—its protection! (*He is convulsed with derisive laughter*)

Matilda laughs scornfully

(*crossing down* R) Well, we'll soon see what it's protection's worth! (*Sees bottle of "Lion-cub Mixture" on the mound*) Hello, what's this? (*He picks up bottle and reads label*) Look Matilda, it's the little lion-cub's Mixture. Oh, I must taste this—very strengthening I believe. (*Uncorks bottle*) He won't last long if I drink the lot! (*Lifts bottle to his lips*)

Matilda Now be careful, Joseph—you know how easily you get upset!

Joseph Oh, that's all right. "Down the hatch!" (*Takes a swig from bottle, then hastily spits it out, making a face and coughing violently*) Oh, Oh, Matilda—it's bitter—bitter! Oh, I think I'm poisoned! (*Dances round coughing and spitting*)

Matilda What does the label say, Joseph?

Joseph (*reads label*) "Caution—for Lion-cubs only." Oh, what a good thing I didn't swallow more of it! (*Flings bottle back on mound—looks off* R) Well, at any rate the children can't be far off.

Matilda (*grimly*) Wait till I catch them! (*She shakes her fist*)

Joseph (*looking off* R) Ah, ah, I think I see someone behind that tree! (*He beckons to Matilda. Matilda moves to* L *of Joseph and looks off* R)

Matilda Why, it's dear little Rosamund.

Joseph And our dear nephew Crispian. (*He calls*) I can see you—running away from your dear kind Uncle Joseph, who has come all this way to fetch you back again. (*He turns to Matilda*) Come and see the little darlings, Matilda.

Matilda Little wretches, I'll make them pay for this.

Joseph Have you got the rope I gave you, Matilda?

Matilda (*patting her bag*) Yes, I've got the rope.

Joseph Good. We'll tie their hands and feet together—so much safer that way—and the gags for their pretty little mouths?

Matilda (*easing* RC) Yes. I've got the gags!

Joseph I never could bear to see children cry—and they might, you know. Just a little. (*He flourishes his whip*)

Matilda (*rubbing her hands with glee*) Just a little!

Joseph Because Uncle Joseph has brought his whip with him to tickle them up for running away. (*He cracks the whip and catches Matilda round the ankles*)

Matilda (*with a screech*) Oh, do be careful, Joseph! (*Rubs her ankle*)

Joseph (*pirouetting and calling to the children off* R) Peek-a-boo! I can see you!

Matilda (*dancing*) Peek-a-boo! Peek-a-boo!

Joseph (*pirouetting*) Come and play with Uncle Joseph!

Matilda (*with a fantastic dance step*) Come and play with Aunt Matilda!

Joseph SSH! They're coming this way!

Joseph and Matilda dance a fairy frolic then exit up L. *There is a slight* **16** *pause. Then Cubs enters* R *on the mound. He looks around, then beckons off. Crispian enters* R *on the mound. He and Cubs step off the mound, move* C *and look cautiously around*

Crispian Have they gone, Cubs?

Cubs nods

(*He calls*) It's all right. They've gone.

Rosamund, Jim and Betty enter down R. *Cubs eases down* LC

Rosamund (*moving* RC *fearfully*) It was Aunt Matilda.
Crispian And Uncle Joseph. He must have got a piece of carpet after all.
Jim (*crossing below Rosamund to* R *of Crispian*) And got the Dragon King
to come after us. I say, we're in for it!
Betty (*moving to* R *of Rosamund*) How dreadful!

Joseph and Matilda, unseen by children, enter up L *and creep down above*
them

Crispian I wish we could have heard what they were saying.
Joseph (*raising his whip: cynically*) Ah, here's your dear kind Uncle
Joseph come all this way to fetch you back again!

Betty and Rosamund scream and cower down R. *Crispian and Jim break* **17**
to LC. *Cubs stands, growling, in front of girls. There is a blinding flash of*
light and St George appears R *on the mound under flag. He has his drawn*
sword in his hand

St George Hold! (*In stern anger, to Joseph*) Behold the power at which
you scoff. Advance one step to harm those I defend, and you will have to
face their champion. (*He points his sword at Joseph and Matilda*)

Joseph and Matilda, terrified, retreat trembling up L. *St George lifts his*
sword and salutes the children. There is a flash as he exits R

Jim Phew! That was a near thing.
Crispian Touch and go.

The children group C. *The sun is setting in a red glow and the light is dimming*

Rosamund Well, at all events, we're quite safe here on St George's ground.
Jim Well I think we ought to prepare for the night.
Crispian Yes. We ought to have a fire. I have some matches.
Jim Let's go and get some wood.
Rosamund Yes, and Betty and I will gather some strawberries. (*She points*
off R) *I saw lots over there.*
Crispian All right.
Rosamund (*moving* R) Come, Betty.

Betty rubs her eyes and hangs her head

What's the matter?
Betty I'm so sleepy.
Crispian (*putting his arm round her*) Poor kid! No wonder she's tired.
Can't you get the strawberries, Rosamund?
Rosamund Of course. But we can't leave Betty here alone.
Crispian No, I forgot that.
Jim Why not? She'll be quite safe.
Rosamund I know! We'll leave Cubs to take care of her.

Cubs crosses to mound

(*She leads Betty to mound*) Betty, lie down there.

Betty lies on mound

Now, Cubs, (*She points to Betty*) Trust! Die at post, but never leave it!

Cubs sits up on trust and growls understandingly

Isn't he a darling?

Cubs lies down close to Betty, with his head on her frock

You'll stay here, Betty? Remember, don't go off the light green ground.
The wood is full of dangers.

Jim Yes, and dangers we must face alone. There'll be no St George to help
us in the wood.

Rosamund (*with a sigh*) No. That's just the awful part of it.

Crispian and Jim move up R

But you're quite safe here, darling. We shan't be long.

Crispian ⎱ No, we shan't be long, Betty.
Jim ⎰

Rosamund exits down R. *Crispian and Jim exit up* R. *The instant they have
gone, Betty sits up and looks around with mischievous eyes, all alert. A
Woodmouse enters down* L *crosses to* L *of mound, sees Betty and Cubs and* **18**
falls flat with fright, squeaks, jumps up and exits hurriedly down L. *Cubs
rises and looks anxiously at Betty. The twitter of fairies is heard off* L.
Dunks enters up L. *He beckons off* L *to the Fairies and Elves, who then enter*
L *led by the Fairy Queen. Dunks exits up* L. *The Fairies are dressed as
different flower-blossoms. Led by the Fairy Queen, the Fairies dance to
Betty, who is entranced. Cubs does not like the Fairies, and sensing danger,
he sits uneasily below the mound and from time to time looks anxiously in
the direction in which Rosamund has gone. The light is still fading as the
sun sets. The Fairies cannot go on to St George's ground and their object is
to lure Betty from it into the wood. They dance to Betty, their arms out-
stretched, inviting her to dance with them. Betty claps her hands with glee
and with a gurgle of delight, rises, jumps off the mound, runs to the Fairies
and dances with them. The dance takes her nearer and nearer to the wood* L.
*Cubs sees her danger and at last can endure it no longer. With a growl he
runs amongst the Fairies, scatters them in all directions, and despite her
struggles, pushes Betty backwards to safety on the mound. She sits down
with a bump on the* L *side of the mound and her feet go up in the air. She
is furious and slaps Cubs as hard as she can. Cubs whimpers and sits below
mound with his face in his paws. The Fairies form again and now Green and
Red Elves join the dance, and again Betty joins them. She runs into their
midst and climbs on the mushroom. Cubs distracted, runs up and down on
the mound, looking off* R *hoping the others will return. He begs Betty to
return to safety, but heedless Betty dances on, enchanted with the smiling
Fairies, never noticing that as she dances with them they are slowly luring
her into the Dragon Wood. As she enters the wood with the Fairies and*

*Elves, one of her shoes drops off. As at last they disappear L with her into
the wood, the Fairies and Elves laugh with impish glee. It grows darker,
Cubs, distracted, runs up and down R and howls piteously. He crosses to
L, howls, sees Betty's shoe, picks it up, sniffs it, then drops it, and with a
last despairing howl, exits L into wood. Rosamund enters down R. She
carries some strawberries on a dock-leaf*

Rosamund (*as she enters*) Look, Betty, I've got some lovely strawberries.
(*She puts the strawberries on the mound and looks around in surprise that
Betty and Cubs are not there. She calls*) Betty! (*She moves up R and calls
again*) Betty! (*She becomes alarmed, runs across to L, sees Betty's shoe,
picks it up and realizes with horror what has happened. She calls de-
sparingly*) Betty! Betty! Where are you? Betty!

*She enters the wood L still calling. The sun has now set and the light is very
dim. Crispian and Jim enter up R. They are whistling, and each carry a
bundle of sticks*

Crispian (*moving down RC*) Well, we'll soon get a fire going now. (*He drops
his bundle of sticks*)
Jim (*moving to R of Crispian*) You bet! (*He drops his bundle of sticks
alongside Crispian's*)
Crispian (*looking around*) Hullo, they're not here.
Jim (*looking around*) Not here?
Crispian Where can they have got to?
Jim I wonder?
Crispian (*anxiously*) Nothing can have happened to them, surely?
Jim Of course not.

Rosamund is heard to call off in the distance L

Rosamund (*off*) Betty! Betty! Betty!
Crispian (*looking L; horror-stricken*) They're in the wood!
Jim (*looking L; horror-stricken*) Yes. And it's sunset!

*Unseen by Crispian and Jim, Dunks enters stealthily up L and stands
watching them*

Crispian Yes—sunset!

The sound of mocking laughter from the Elves and Fairies is heard off L

*Crispian and Jim grip hands, then with determination cross and exit into
wood down L. Dunks, with a triumphant hiss, moves down L, then follows
the boys off, as the* CURTAIN *falls*

The CURTAIN *rises again, and St George, with his drawn sword in his hand,
is seen standing on the mound, facing L as though keeping guard over the
children*

CURTAIN

ACT III

SCENE 1

The Witch's Cove. Sunset

The scene is a shallow, with a background depicting a small, rocky cove in the seashore, with caves and dark cliffs. There are high rocks RC *and* LC *and entrances* R *and* L

As the CURTAIN *rises Will runs on and dances solo to his shadow*

At the end of the dance, Will exits R

There is a peal of thunder as the Witch flies on R. *As she moves* RC *John*
Carey and Vera, his wife, enter L. *Carey is a strongly built, soldierly-looking man of about thirty-five. He wears a frayed pair of flannel trousers and a torn shirt. He is without a jacket. Vera, very beautiful, is younger than Carey. Her hair is down and her dress is patched and frayed. She stands* L *as Carey crosses to* C

Carey (*to the Witch, angrily*) You here again? Be off with you! I warned you I'd not have you hanging about.

Witch (*cringing*) Oh, why so vexed with the poor Witch? What harm has she done you?

Carey Harm! You evil creature. Why, you're very presence is enough. Clear out—at once!

Witch (*in wheedling tones*) Have patience and the Witch will tell you what your heart desires to hear.

Carey (*threateningly*) You shall tell me nothing. Be off!

Witch (*hobbling to* R *of Carey*) Oh, hot blood, hot blood! You go too fast. Listen! A storm I brewed did harrass a fair ship for England bound.

Vera reacts

As I leapt ashore, so leapt the waves about her, mountainous, stupendous. As I shrieked, so shrieked the tempest—she reeled, she staggered—as I ashore did reel and reel—and dance about the bubbling pot. He! He! He!

Carey Here, that's enough! (*He turns and moves* LC) Be off with you!

Vera (*crossing to* R *of Carey*) Darling, let her speak. (*To the Witch*) You say the ship was bound for England?

Witch (*moving to* R *of Vera*) The pretty one is curious?

Vera retreats a step

The Witch's frolic o'er doth find the ship afloat and whole, blown from her course. (*She points* L) And there—beyond the cliffs—she rides at anchor, searching this shore for sign of habitants.

Vera Beyond the cliffs? Oh, are you telling us the truth?
Witch (*menacingly*) I'll tell you nothing. (*She turns from Vera and raises* **23**
her arm) Master, thy bidding's done.

She flies off R

Vera (*crossing and looking up the cliffs* L) A ship. A ship—out there!
Carey (*moving to* R *of Vera*) It's a lie—to torture us with hope.
Vera (*turning and crossing to* C) But *if* it's true—they may rescue us—and
we shall see our children again.
Carey (*moving to* L *of Vera*) Dearest, you mustn't believe her. (*He puts his
arm consolingly around Vera's shoulders and leads her to the rock* RC)
Remember she is a creature of the evil power that rules this land. (*He
sits on the rock* BC) What good can we expect of her?

Vera kneels beside Carey

If you and I weren't in such a hopeless fix ourselves, they wouldn't have
left us in peace so long. Cheer up, darling, we still have each other.
Vera (*embracing Carey*) I know, I know—but our children, Rosamund and
Crispian—what will become of them? John darling, do go up the cliffs
and look. Suppose the Witch *was* speaking the truth?
Carey My poor darling, it's ten to one she's hiding in some cavern over
there and laughing at us.
Vera But suppose there is a ship! (*She rises*) Oh, if only I were able, even
on so small a chance (*She moves* C) I'd climb the cliff—and all the time
my heart would cry "Rosamund, Crispian, mother's coming to you—
mother's coming to you."
Carey (*rising*) Dearest. (*He moves to* R *of Vera and puts his arm round her*)
There, there, I'll go.

Vera looks up joyfully

But while I'm gone, promise me, don't be too hopeful. (*He crosses to* L) **24**

The sound of Will's pipe is heard faintly off R

Carey (*stops and turns*) What's that?
Vera That's Will.
Carey The rascal. I wonder what mischief he's been up to.
Vera Oh, he's not a bad little fellow—and you can't expect perfection in a
Will-o'-the-Wisp.
Carey (*laughing*) And of course you can't believe a word he says.
Vera (*easing* RC) I don't know what I should have done without him. He
knows all the legends of this strange country—and has even seen pilgrims
on their way to where the rainbow ends.
Carey (*incredulously*) Where the rainbow ends? I'm afraid that's only one
of Will's yarns.
Vera Oh, but he says he knows the way—and that it lies beyond the
Thundercloud Mountains.   **25**

The sound of Will's pipe is heard

Carey (*moving to* L *of Vera*) Well, true or not, his tales amuse you; and
I'm glad he will be with you while I'm gone. Goodbye, sweetheart. (*He
kisses Vera*) I won't be long. (*He moves* L) And don't forget how often I
have brought you back disappointment.
Vera But there *may* be a ship . . .

Carey makes a despairing gesture and exits L. *Vera sits pensively on the* **26**
rock LC. *Will enters* R

*He dances and pipes. Vera, absorbed in her thoughts, does not notice him.
After a while Will stops and looks at Vera reproachfully. He pipes a little,
but Vera is still oblivious to him*

Will (*angrily*) Mother Vera! (*He stamps his foot*) Will's here!   **27**
Vera (*looking at Will; with a smile*) Oh, Will. I didn't hear you. I was
listening.
Will Listening? Listening? Listening for what?
Vera (*ecstatically*) For the sound of a cheer echoing across the waters—to
the cry of voices far away, who cry "Mother, we want you".
Will (*who has been dancing, stopping short*) "Mother, we want you?"
Why, that's what the children said today, who are trying to find their
father and mother where the rainbow ends. (*He dances again*)
Vera Children? Not children, Will?
Will Yes, much children. All children. (*He counts on his fingers*) One, two,
three, four. (*He dances to* R) Two boy-beasts . . . (*He pipes and dances
to* C) and two girl-beasts.
Vera (*rising and moving to* L *of Will*) Children? You must have made a
mistake! (*She crosses below Will to* RC) No child could ever make such
a journey.

Will pipes and dances to L

Will, are you sure you are speaking the truth?
Will (*dancing*) Truth—much truth. Will very good today (*he dances to* C)
Oh, very, very, very, *very* good today (*dances*)
Vera What can it mean? (*She coaxes Will*) Will, come and sit by Mother
Vera (*she sits on the rock* RC) and tell her story of children going to where
the raindow ends.
Will No! Will not sit—(*he flits to* L) Will fly!
Vera (*craftily coaxing Will*) Will very clever today. Tell Mother Vera
story. Will *very* clever.
Will (*moving* C, *flattered*) Will very clever. Very, very, very, *very* clever
today. (*He runs to* L *of Vera*) Will tell Mother Vera all about it.

Vera tries to catch hold of Will. He evades Vera and flits to C. *Vera holds
out her hands to him, he runs to* L *of Vera and kneels beside her*

Will met man and woman in the wood—very bad man and woman. Will
listen to them talking. They want to catch children—so Will led them

into bog—very, very bad bog (*he rises*) hope they die there! (*He flits to* L)
Will *very* clever! (*He dances to* C)

Vera (*despairingly*) But the children, Will?

Will (*dancing to* R) Oh! (*He flits to* C) Will heard children talking outside
wood. Will like children girl-beasts very, very much. Girl-beasts talk
soft—like doves—so—"Rosamund—Betty—Betty—Rosamund".

Vera (*rising*) *Rosamund!*

Will Nice beast, Rosamund. Golden hair—like the sun. Blue eyes—like
the sky.

Vera (*excitedly*) Golden hair—blue eyes . . . And the boys, did they talk?

Will Will not like boy-beasts—not much! Boy-beasts talk like this (*he
imitates Jim*) "Crispian—"

Vera *Crispian!*

Will "That's a Will-o'-the-Wisp—let's catch him" Will fly away then. Not
like boy-beasts.

Vera (*earnestly trying to capture Will's attention*) Crispian! You're sure it
was Crispian and Rosamund?

Will (*carelessly*) Sure—much sure. They come to find father and mother
where the rainbow ends (*He dances to* L)

Vera realizes that Will has seen her children and moves C

But they can't fly. Perhaps wild beasts eat them soon (*He dances to* L *of* **28**
Vera) Will not care—Will safe—Will fly!

Vera (*catching hold of Will*) Will, Will, listen. Don't be frightened; I won't
hurt you. These children whom you saw are mine—I'm sure of it.

Will All? (*Counts on his fingers*) One, two, three, four?

Vera No, Rosamund and Crispian—they are mine. They have come to
find their father and me. (*Earnestly*) Will, you know the way. You must
take me to where the rainbow ends.

Will But Mother Vera cannot fly like Will. (*He dances* L) Children gone
before she gets there.

Vera (*in agony of mind*) What shall I do? What shall I do? (*She sinks to
her knees and puts her hands to her face*)

Carey (*off* L *calling*) Ship ahoy! Ship ahoy!

The sound of distant cheers is heard off L

Vera (*looking up, spellbound*) A ship! (*She rises*)

Will jumps on to the rock LC *and looks off* L

Will A ship! A ship—that flies like bird. Ship take Mother Vera to where
the rainbow ends. (*He jumps from the rock and moves to* L *of Vera*) Will
know the way. (*He takes Vera by the hand*)

Carey (*off* L *calling*) Castaways—ahoy—ahoy!

Will leads Vera L, *and as they exit the Lights Black-out*

CURTAIN

SCENE 2

The Dragon's Wood. Evening

The scene is of a dark woodland, with a back-cloth depicting part of a lake **29**
*with a boggy shore. An old, gnarled tree, with just a suggestion of a human
form and face, stands* C. *It has two branches, in the form of sleeves, so that
the operator, concealed inside the tree, is able to catch and hold the players:
and there is a small peep-hole in the front of the tree through which the
operator can see the stage*

When the CURTAIN *rises a Frog is squatting* R *of the tree. The sound of
mocking elfin laughter is heard off. Will enters up* R. *He runs round the stage
playing a warning call on his pipe. The Frog hastily hops to* L *and exits. Will
follows him off. The laughter ceases, and the Black Bear enters up* R. *He
lumbers across the stage in time to the music and hurries off down* L. *An Elf
appears from behind the tree. He carries a lantern. He looks to* L *and* R, *runs
round behind the tree and comes down* C. *A Woodmouse enters up* L *with Will,
Elves with lanterns, and Fairies enter* R *and* L

The Woodmouse crosses to the tree, sits R *of it and brushes her whiskers. Will
pipes merrily in the background. Frogs enter* R *and* L *and dance with Elves and
Fairies. Woodmouse joins in. One of the Fairies, passing too close in front
of the tree, is caught by one of its branches. She screams and the Elves rescue
her. Will runs down* C *and exits, piping a warning note. The Dancers form a
hushed gathering on the* R. *Betty enters up* L *dragged and pushed by the Elves,
who pinch her, pull her hair and tease her. They laugh shrilly and mock her as
they bring her down* C. *She wears only one shoe and her sash is untied, and she is
desperate and harrassed. The other Elves and Fairies all join in tormenting her*

Betty (*stamping her foot*) Go away, you horrid little things!

The Elves laugh shrilly, point their fingers at Betty and continue to tease her

First Elf Let's pinch her, comrades, black and blue.

*Elves and Fairies swarm round Betty jostling each other to get close enough
to pinch her*

Elves Yes—yes—let's pinch her!
Betty Oh, no, no, no! You're very, very mean—so many to just me.

The Elves jeer at Betty

Second Elf Let's take her shoe. The Woodmouse wants a cradle for her
son. (*He drags Betty's shoe from her foot and tosses it down* R)

*They all run at Betty again. She tries desperately to pass them, but they join
hands and dance around her in a circle and sing*

All   You can't escape us, no, no, no!
                           The sun has set, the owl cries so,
                           Tu-whit, tu-whit, tu-whoo!

> A child caught here when sun is low,
> Is pinched by us all black and blue
> From dainty head to toe.

Cubs enter down L

Betty (*seeing Cubs*) Cubs! Cubs!

Cubs runs at the Elves, Fairies and Frogs, scatters them and chases them all off R *and* L *with the exception of one Frog, who hides behind the tree. The Frog peeps out at Cubs, who sees him and runs at him with a growl. The Frog jumps over Cubs and exits hurriedly* L. *Cubs runs to* L *of Betty*

(*She pats Cubs thankfully. Tearfully*) Thank you, Cubs darling. I was *so* frightened. (*She moves down* R *and picks up her shoe. In distress*) Oh, Mummy! Mummy!

She exits down R *with Cubs. There is a short pause, then Crispian and Jim enter* L. *Jim limps a little. Crispian has his handkerchief tied round his hand. Both look dishevelled and dirty and their clothes are torn*

Crispian (*crossing quickly to* R *and looking off*) I thought I heard Betty's voice. (*He turns and moves* RC) It must have been the Elves, they're everywhere.

Jim stands down L

Where *can* the girls be?

The Slitherslime crawls in up L. *It is a loathesome creature with a worm-shaped, hairless head. It has a gaping, loose-lipped mouth and its large staring eyes are blind. Dragging its useless, flabby legs behind it, it crawls below the tree* LC

Jim (*pointing to the Slitherslime*) Look!
Crispian It's a Slitherslime!
Jim It must have crawled up from the marshes. How horrible!

They watch in horror as the Slitherslime crawls up R *and exits. The howl of the Hyenas is heard off* L. *Jim and Crispian exchange glances. Jim crosses to* R

What's that? (*He looks off* R)
Crispian (*crossing to* L *and looking off*) Hyenas. The wood is full of wild animals. (*He backs slowly to* C) If we hadn't set fire to that bush when we did that leopard would have made short work of us.
Jim (*looking off* R *backing to* C) He caught my heel as it was, the brute. (*As he looks intently off* R *he backs into Crispian who is looking off* L. *Without looking round, both yell and rush to take cover on opposite sides of the*

tree C. *Jim to* R *of it and Crispian to* L *of it. They raise their fists and cautiously creep round the tree towards each other, and meet face to face. They both laugh at their own nervousness*

Jim (*moves down* C) I say, I'm hungry, aren't you?

Crispian Starving! And to think of the girls—alone—it's awful (*he crosses to* R) if only we could find them. (*He looks off* R)

Jim There are so many paths in this confounded wood.

Crispian (*crossing below the tree and calling off* L) Rosamund, hullo! hullo!

Jim (*looking off* R) Look out, Cris! (*He points off* R) There's something moving over there in the trees.

Crispian (*moving down* LC) Where?

Jim (*pointing off* R) There!

The Slacker enters R. *He is a tall, thin youth, a little older than Jim and Crispian, with a slightly decadent air. He is round-shouldered and walks with a slouch. His face is livid and he has a tired, blasé air. He speaks with a bored accent. He is dressed in a green doublet and hose with a green dragon embroidered on the left breast. He carries a fishing-basket slung over his shoulder. A green light follows him wherever he goes*

Slacker (*moving* RC) Hullo, you chaps! You look as though you'd been in the wars a bit. (*Points to Crispian's hand*)

Crispian (*moving down* R *of tree*) Oh! Nothing much.

Jim Only a scratch. (*Moves down* L *of the tree*)

Slacker (*with a bored air*) Well, it's more than I'd like to own to. (*He yawns and throws himself on the ground as if the act of standing was insupportable. Looks them up and down*) Going to where the rainbow ends, aren't you?

Crispian (*with a look at Jim*) Yes. But how did you know? Who are you?

Slacker (*yawns*) They call me the Slacker. I once started for where the rainbow ends.

Jim
Crispian } (*together*) You did?

Slacker Yes—I'd lost a sister and wanted to find her . . .

Crispian (*eagerly*) And did you get there?

Slacker No fear, too tough for me! To say nothing of the danger. Besides, I got horribly hungry.

Jim and Crispian exchange glances

So I just stayed here. (*Yawns and lies back*)

Jim
Crispian } (*together*) Stayed here?

Slacker (*propping himself up on his elbow, watching them covertly*) Yes, why not? It's a jolly fine place—(*meaningly*)—if you're lucky enough to find someone to put you wise to it—someone like myself, see? (*He rises and picks up fishing-basket*) No work to do. No one to boss you around. Plenty to eat—(*he crosses and stands between Jim and Crispian*)—and as for fishing—(*he opens basket*)—look at these!

Crispian (*peering into basket*) What splendid trout!
Jim (*looking into basket*) Did you catch them yourself?
Slacker Yes. (*He closes basket*) I netted them. (*He slings basket over his shoulder*) There are masses of them in the lake.

Crispian and Jim look eager. The Slacker takes note of the impression he has made

Slacker (*temptingly*) You'd be surprised the things there are to do here—
that *I* could show you . . . (*Makes a movement with his head towards* R)
What d'you say? Will you come with me?

Jim and Crispian make a movement towards him. A Hyena howls off

Jim (*checking*) But what about the wild beasts?
Crispian Yes, they must be jolly awkward.
Slacker Not a bit of it! (*Beckons them to him*) Have you noticed a green
light about me?
Jim   ⎫ (*together*) Yes!
Crispian ⎭
Slacker Well, no beast dare come near it—it's Dragon Light!
Jim   ⎫ (*recoiling*) Dragon Light?
Crispian ⎭
Slacker Yes, I pay the Dragon King toll for it—to protect me.
Crispian Pay for it? How?
Slacker (*yawning*) Oh, I just give him my letters, unopened, that the
pilgrims bring me from home.
Crispian Your letters—*unopened*!
Jim Your parents' letters?
Crispian What a rotten thing to do!
Slacker (*leaning against the tree, quite unmoved, indifferently*) Oh, I don't
know—I don't care. When you've eaten Dragon Fruit you're never sorry
for anything.

The boys look askance at the Slacker

And smashing grub it is too! (*He takes two rosy apples from his basket
and holds them out enticingly to the boys*) Have some?

Jim and Crispian stretch out their hands eagerly, then withdraw

Slacker (*temptingly*) Come on! You're hungry aren't you? There's nothing
to be afraid of . . . try it.

Jim and Crispian each take a fruit. The Slitherslime enters up R *and crawls
slowly above the tree to* L *of it*

Jim (*in sudden fear, just as Crispian is about to bite fruit*) Stop!
Slacker (*angrily*) What's up? (*He crosses to* L *of Jim*) Why shouldn't he?
Jim (*deliberately*) What do we have to pay the Dragon King if we eat?
Slacker (*shrugging his shoulders, casually*) Nothing much. (*He indicates*

the Dragon crest on his breast) You'd have to wear this.
Jim And what's the end of it all?
Slacker (*indicating the Slitherslime*) *That!* (*He laughs hysterically*)

Jim and Crispian recoil in horror and hastily throw their fruit off R *and* L.
Jim crosses to L *of Crispian and clasps his hand.*
The Slitherslime exits up L

Slacker (*very angry*) Well! Of all the silly young fools. Well, play it the
hard way if you want to, but I warn you, you'll be jolly hungry before
you get to your journey's end—and how do you know that you'll ever
get to where the rainbow ends?
Crispian (*desperately*) Well, at any rate, we're going to have a jolly good
try.
Slacker (*sneering*) That's because you've no idea what you're up against.
This forest stretches for miles, and even if the wild beasts don't get you
you'll probably be drowned in the lake—many chaps are.
Crispian Well, that's no excuse for chucking our hand in now, is it
Blunders?
Jim Of course not!

The green light on Slacker starts to fade

Slacker Why not? What's the use of trying if you can't win?
Jim Because at least then we'll know we've done our best.

The green light on Slacker fades completely

Slacker (*collapsing in terror*) Stop! Stop!
Crispian (*to Jim*) Look, the green light's gone!
Slacker It cannot burn because you have called up the influence of an
ideal! Leave me! Leave me! I shall be eaten by the beasts! (*Crouches on
ground in abject fear*)
Crispian (*crossing to* R *of the Slacker*) No, come with us—we'll get through
somehow.
Jim (*crossing to* R *of Crispian*) Yes—come with us!
Slacker Come with you—(*then backing away*)—to fight—to work—
perhaps to starve—*never!*

The green light reappears

I'll stay here!

The green light grows stronger

(*he laughs hysterically*) The Dragon Light! It's coming back! It's
getting brighter! I'm saved! I'm saved!

He laughs hysterically and exits down L

Crispian Poor chap, he's done for.
Jim Well, it's no use worrying about him. If only we could find the girls!

Crispian Rather! (*He crosses to* RC *and points off* R) Let's try this path.

Cubs enters down R *and runs joyfully to Crispian*

Why, it's Cubs!

Cubs runs down R *beckons to Crispian and points off down* R

Jim (*crossing to Crispian*) What's he doing?

Crispian moves down R *and looks off*

Jim (*joyfully*) Look—there's Betty! (*Calling*) Betty! Betty!

He exits quickly down R *still calling, followed by Crispian and Cubs*

There is a short pause, then enter Will L
    He is bubbling with laughter and mischief. He runs to R *of the tree, peeps out towards* L, *and imitates Matilda's voice*

Will (*enjoying himself*) Joseph, Joseph, where are you, Joseph?

A groan is heard off L *then enter Joseph down* L. *He is in a pitiable state, having fallen into a bog and his clothes are torn. He looks thoroughly dishevelled and miserable. He has lost his whip, but still carries his top-hat very much the worse for wear*

Joseph (*moving* C *testily*) Where are you, Matilda? (*He moves* R)
Will (*silently clapping his hands, skips around above the tree and peeps out* L *of it—imitating Matilda's voice*) Here! Here!
Joseph (*turning; bewildered*) Where, where? (*He crosses to* LC)

Will, delighted, skips around above the tree and peeps out R *of it*

Will (*imitating Matilda's voice*) Here! Here!
Joseph (*turning*) Where, where? (*He crosses to* R)

Will hides above tree

Have you fallen down a rabbit hole? (*He moves up* R)

Will hides L *of the tree*

I'll send a ferret down for you.

Still grumbling to himself he exits R

Will moves below the tree. He shakes with laughter and claps his hands with glee. He then flits to R *of the tree, peeps out towards* L *and imitates Joseph's voice*

Will Matilda, Matilda, where are you, Matilda?

Groans are heard and Matilda enters down L. *Her dress and petticoat are*

torn. She has lost her toupee and her hair is in disarray. She still wears her scarf and carries her bag

Matilda (*crossing wearily to* RC) Joseph, Joseph, where are you, Joseph?

Will skips around above the tree and peeps out L *of it*

Will (*imitating Joseph's voice*) Here! Here!

Matilda turns, crosses and looks off L

Joseph enters R, *grumbling to himself, and while looking off* R *backs down* C

Joseph What a tiresome woman you are, Matilda.

Matilda, still looking off L, *backs down* C

If you've lost yourself, do try and find yourself! Wherever are you?

As Joseph and Matilda back towards each other, Will comes from his hiding place and dodges between them

Will (*mockingly*) Cuckoo! Cuckoo!

He runs down C, *crosses below Matilda, and exits down* L

Joseph and Matilda collide. Matilda shrieks and turns

Joseph (*turning*) So there you are—you—midsummer night's dream.
Matilda (*pointing off* L) It was that Will-o'-the-Wisp that led us into the bog.
Joseph Such a nasty smelly bog too (*he looks ruefully at his clothes*) it's quite spoilt my suit.
Matilda (*pointing* L) Let's try this path. (*She moves* LC)

Joseph starts to follow Matilda, treads on a piece of her trailing dress and tears it further

Matilda (*stops and turns*) There! You've torn my dress.
Joseph (*laughing*) Never mind, we'll split the difference.
Matilda Just look at you! Your trousers—they *will* want pressing.

Joseph sits on the ground C *below the tree and leans back against it, wearily*

Joseph It's the thorns in this wood—they're terrible.

The tree snatches Joseph's hat off his head, then quickly replaces it

(*alarmed*) Matilda, what's that?

The Tree waves it's arms over Joseph's head

Matilda (*with a scream*) Look out, Joseph! The tree—it's alive!

Joseph hastily scrambles to his feet, moves to R *of Matilda, takes off his hat and starts to polish it*

Oh, let's get out of this dreadful place! (*She turns and moves* L. *Then stops, and looks off* L. *Excitedly*) Joseph! Joseph!

Joseph (*intent on his hat*) What is it?

Matilda (*turning and pulling Joseph round to face* L) Look—Rosamund!

Joseph (*looking off* L) So it is! (*He puts on his hat*) Dear little Rosamund: and coming this way, too. (*He moves* C *and rubs his hands gleefully*) What a bit of luck for us! We couldn't have ventured out there again with that nasty St George on duty—and his sword too.

Matilda (*moving to* L *of Joseph*) Such a nasty sharp sword! (*She takes the rope from her bag*)

Joseph What a pity I dropped my whip! But I see you've got the rope, Matilda.

Matilda (*meaningly*) Yes, I've got the rope.

Joseph And something to gag their pretty little mouths.

Matilda (*patting her bag, grimly*) I've got the gags.

Joseph Good. (*He leads Matilda below the tree*) You remember the Dragon King told us that hyenas roam the wood in search of prey at moonrise?

Matilda (*with a shudder, looking nervously around*) It must be nearly that now.

Joseph (*rubbing his hands*) Yes. I think when we catch dear little Rosamund, we'll tie her to this tree—and then we'll go away, you and I. I never could bear to hear children cry—and the hyenas might make her cry a little.

Matilda Just a little!

Joseph It's a funny little way they have with children.

He and Matilda laugh. The tree suddenly snatches Matilda's scarf and puts it into the hole in its trunk. Matilda shrieks

Matilda (*breaking* LC) My scarf! The monster—it's eaten my scarf!

Joseph sees the scarf disappearing into the tree trunk and makes a rush at it, but receives a nasty knock from the tree. He steps back a pace or two

Joseph Petty larceny in the wood, eh? Seven days without option. (*He moves cautiously to the tree and smacks it*) You naughty, naughty, tree!

The tree reaches and knocks Joseph over. Joseph rises and the tree hits him again. Joseph staggers RC

Matilda (*moving to the tree and shaking her fist at it*) You ought to be ashamed of yourself—taking my scarf.

The tree makes a pass at Matilda

She screams and moves quickly LC   30

It'll be taking my dress next!

Rosamund (*off* L *calling, wearily*) Betty! Betty!

Joseph (*to Matilda*) Ssh—Rosamund! We'll hide behind this tree and jump on her unawares. (*He and Matilda hide above the tree*)

Rosamund enters L. *She looks weary and dishevelled and her dress is torn. She carries Betty's shoe*

Rosamund (*crossing to* C *calling*) Betty! Betty!

Matilda jumps out from R *of tree and bars Rosamund's path. Rosamund screams and turns to run* L. *Joseph jumps out from* L *of the tree and bars her path. Rosamund shrieks in terror and drops Betty's shoe*

Joseph (*grabbing Rosamund's left arm*) So Uncle Joseph has found his little girlie at last!

Matilda grabs Rosamund's right arm. She and Joseph drag Rosamund backwards to the tree

Rosamund (*shrieking*) Let me go! Let me go!
Joseph Give me the rope, Matilda.

Matilda hands rope to Joseph

Uncle Joseph will bind her to this tree.
Rosamund (*struggling*) No! No! Let me go! Let me go!

Matilda holds Rosamund while Joseph binds her wrists. He takes the rope and runs around the tree. As he does so he catches Matilda round the neck with it and half strangles her

Matilda (*choking*) Joseph, Joseph—do be careful! (*She disentangles herself*)

Joseph finishes tying the rope. Rosamund is paralysed with terror

Joseph (*surveying Rosamund*) So much safer that way.

The howl of the Hyenas is heard in the distance off L

Matilda (*terrified*) The hyenas! Coming this way. Quick, let us go!
Rosamund (*in terror; calling*) Crispian! Crispian! Help! Help!
Matilda (*taking the gag from her bag*) This will silence her. (*She moves to Rosamund and gags her*)

The howl of the Hyenas is heard nearer off L

(*She catches Joseph by the arm and drags him* RC) Come, come—or we shall be caught!
Joseph (*pointing at Rosamund*) *This* will give them a little diversion. (*To Rosamund*) What a pity isn't it that brother Crispian is in the wood and you can't call him to help you?

The howl of the Hyenas is heard off L; *nearer this time. Matilda tugs frantically at Joseph's arm*

And when he does come I'm afraid you won't be here—the hyenas are so fond of little children.

The howls of the Hyenas are heard loudly off L. *Joseph and Matilda exit hurriedly* R. *Rosamund struggles violently, then her head droops in despair*

Crispian, Jim, Betty and Cubs enter up R

All (*ad lib*) Rosamund—Rosamund!

They all cross slowly up L *above the tree, searching and calling for Rosamund. She attempts to call, but owing to the gag, in vain. Her head droops as Crispian, Jim, Betty and Cubs exit up* L. *A Hyena enters down* L *creeps to Rosamund, sniffs her ankles, then turns and exits quickly* L. *Rosamund, terrified, shrinks against the tree. The tree removes the gag from Rosamund's mouth and puts it into the hole in its trunk. This rouses Rosamund who lifts her head and shrieks*

Rosamund (*calling*) Crispian! Crispian! Crispian!

The children's voices are heard calling excitedly up L: *then Cubs enters up* L *and runs to Rosamund. Crispian, Betty and Jim all rush on up* L

Crispian⎫
Betty ⎬ (*as they enter; ad lib*) Rosamund! Where are you? Where are
Jim ⎭ you?

Rosamund (*calling*) I'm here! Help! Help! I'm here, tied to a tree!

Crispian, Betty and Jim run to Rosamund

Betty (*excitedly*) Rosamund! Rosamund!
Jim Tied to a tree!
Crispian Untie her, quick!

They all help to untie Rosamund. Betty sees her shoe, which Rosamund dropped, and puts it on. When Rosamund is free, Crispian puts his arm around her

Jim Who did it?
Rosamund (*tearfully*) It was Uncle Joseph and Aunt Matilda.
Crispian It's all right, you're safe now.

With loud howls the pack of Hyenas enter L. *The girls huddle against the tree. Jim, Crispian and Cubs stand in front of them*

Look, the hyenas. Go for them, Cubs!

The Hyenas move C *and show fight. Cubs heartily joins in and goes for them, helped by the boys. Suddenly the tree takes Matilda's scarf from the hole and flings it amongst the Hyenas. There is a pause as they sniff it, then with renewed howls they all exit* R

Jim (*mystified*) What made them go?
Crispian (*picking up the scarf and holding it up*) This! Aunt Matilda's scarf! (*He laughs*) Jove! They're on her scent!

The howls of Hyenas are heard off R. *Cubs moves* RC *and faces* R

Crispian They're coming back! Let's get out of this quickly. Run! Run! Come on, Cubs.

Rosamund, Betty, Jim, Crispian and Cubs exit hastily L. *There is a pause, then Matilda enters, shrieking,* R *pursued by the Hyenas. She runs across and exits* L *and is followed off by the Hyenas. As they disappear, Joseph, roaring with laughter at Matilda's plight, enters* R. *He stands* RC *pointing after her, doubled up with mirth. The Black Bear, stalking Joseph, enters* R *walking on its hind legs. Joseph moves* C. *The Black Bear, unseen by him, moves above the tree, sits on the ground* L *of it and watches Joseph*

Joseph (*moving to the tree*) Poor old Aunt Matilda—I hope they haven't killed her! (*He sits on the ground below tree*) Ah, well, no funeral expenses—so much cheaper that way. (*He points off* L) One thing, *I'm* perfectly safe. (*He looks around but does not notice the Black Bear, which has come close behind Joseph* L *and hovers over him*) D'you know, there must be a Guardian Angel watching over me. Fancy being afraid of a hyena—well, it was the highest Ena I ever saw. Now, if I met a wild animal—do you know what I'd do? Well, I'd look him straight in the face—I'd double both of my fists—and I'd give it such a smack in the . . .

He turns to demonstrate, sees the Black Bear and rises, terrified. He makes a pass at the Black Bear, who promptly knocks him down. He rises, hits the Black Bear, and is knocked down again. He rises, very politely raises his hat, suddenly hits the Black Bear with it and dodges to R *of the tree and then above it. The Black Bear moves below the tree and turns. Joseph backs round the* L *side of the tree*

The Black Bear bites him

Joseph runs to L

As he does so, the Hyenas enter L, *knock him down, swarm over him with hideous howls and devour him. The Black Bear sits below tree, holds his sides and laughs as*

the Lights Black Out and the CURTAIN *falls*

SCENE 3

The Lake at the End of the Wood   32

This is a very beautiful scene. There are tree wings R *and* L. *The backcloth depicts a beautiful lake, over which the moon shines. The Thundercloud Mountains can be seen in the distance. Across the back of the stage runs the shore of the lake—a grassy bank with stepping-stones leading down from the* R. *Slightly* L *of* C, *grass-covered steps lead down stage to stage level, while*

*upstage more stepping-stones are presumed to lead into the lake. The bank
continues off* L. *The moon is shining over the waters of the lake*

When the CURTAIN *rises Will enters and pipes the Spirit of the Lake from* 33
the lake waters. She rises LC *and comes down the grassy bank and steps. She
is a beautiful maiden dressed in shimmering pale-green draperies, with long,
green locks in which water-lilies are twined*

*Will and the Spirit of the Lake dance together, until they are frightened by
the First and Second Green Dragons, who enter* L *and* R. *The Spirit of the
Lake runs up to the lake and plunges in up* LC. *The First Green Dragon hides
behind a tree wing* L *and the Second Green Dragon hides behind a tree wing*
R. *Will now pipes again and Fairies dressed as water lilies, led by the Fairy
Queen, and Dragon-Flies enter up* R *and* L *and dance a frolic to Will's piping.
At the end of the dance they all exit* R *and* L. *Will exits* R

There is a short pause   34

The Dragon King, followed by Dunks, enters along the bank up L. *Dunks
moves down* L. *The Dragon King stands on the bank up* LC

Dragon King Tell me, have these children been lured into the wood?
Dunks Yes, they have, your Majesty.
Dragon King They cannot escape me now. Here at this ford shall my
    Flying-Dragons descend upon them and carry them to my fortress on
    yonder mountain-top. See this done.
Dunks (*bowing*) It shall be as your Majesty desires.
Dragon King Then go with all despatch, acquaint those in authority with
    my command.

   Dunks exits L

   The moon rides high above the lake: they should be here anon. (*He raises* 35
   his arms above his head)

   The First and Second Green Dragons show themselves R *and* L, *acknow-
   ledge the Dragon King's silent command, then conceal themselves again.
   The Dragon King moves down* LC *and exits* L. *The voices of the children are
   heard off up* R. *They are laughing and talking*

Jim (*off; calling*) Look, a lake!
All (*off; ad lib*) Where? Where?
Crispian (*off*) Out there—through the trees.
All (*off; ad lib*) Quick! Hurry, hurry! The ford! The ford at last!

   Betty, Rosamund, Jim, Crispian and Cubs enter on the stepping-stones up R

Betty Oh, stepping-stones! Do hurry up! (*She points* L) Oh, look,
    mountains!
Rosamund Yes. They must be the Thundercloud Mountains where the
    Dragon King lives.

Crispian Well, let's hurry up. Here goes! (*He moves over the stepping-stones to* C) Yes, it's quite shallow. Come, Rosamund. Shall I give you a hand, Betty?

The light starts to grow dim

Betty (*moving over the stones*) No, thank you, Cris. I'm quite all right. (*She slips and screams*)   36
Crispian There, you nearly slipped. (*He takes Betty's hand and leads her* C)

Jim and Rosamund, followed by Cubs move down the stones and stand LC. *A loud menacing howl is heard off* L

Rosamund What was that?
Crispian (*looking* L) It seemed to come from that cedar tree.
Rosamund How dark the wood looks. I'm thankful we're out of it.   37

A loud growl is heard off down R. *Jim moves down* L *and looks off. Crispian moves down* R *and looks off. Cubs runs from one to the other. The Dragon King enters quietly along the bank up* L *and stands on the bank up* LC. *The First and Second Green Dragons fly down* R *and* L *and pounce on the girls, who scream. The Second Green Dragon seizes Betty and carries her off* L. *The First Green Dragon seizes Rosamund and carries her off* R. *Crispian runs frantically off* R. *after Rosamund. Jim runs off* L *after Betty. Cubs runs back and forward from* R *to* L. *The Dragon King stands up* LC *dominating the scene. Crispian re-enters* R)

Crispian (*crossing and calling off* L) Blunders! Blunders!

The Dragon King raises his arms. The First Red Dragon flies on from R, *seizes Crispian and carries him off* R. *Jim re-enters* L

Jim (*crossing and calling off* R) Crispian! Crispian!

The Second Red Dragon flies on from L, *seizes Jim and carries him off* L. *Cubs runs distractedly from* L *to* R *then exits* R

Dragon King (*raising his arms, exulting*) Victory! Victory is mine!   38

CURTAIN

ACT IV

SCENE 1

The ramparts of the Dragon King's Castle

The castle is built on the topmost crag of the Thundercloud Mountains. An arch up C *leads into the building.* R *of the arch is a tower from the top of which flies the Dragon King's flag. A window in the downstage side of the tower, which can be reached by climbing on the ramparts wall, leads, by way of concealed steps inside, to the platform on which the flagpole is mounted. Running diagonally down* R *from the tower is the outer wall of the ramparts, against which is a throne mounted on a small rostrum. Beyond can be seen the jagged tops of the mountains backed by the sky. The* L *side of the stage is bounded by the solid walls of the castle buildings*

When the CURTAIN *rises, Crispian and Jim, both fettered, stand* C. *Crispian is* R *of Jim. Rosamund and Betty crouch on the steps of the throne. Betty is weeping*

Crispian I say, this is terrible! And the worst of the whole thing is that we should have dragged you two into it.

Jim Don't worry about that. I don't regret it.

Betty (*rising and drying her eyes*) I don't regret it either.

Crispian But they may keep us here for years.

Rosamund We shall all be awfully ignorant.

Crispian I wish we had the Carpet.

Betty Or dear St George to help us.

Rosamund He can't help us here. The book said at the end of our journey nothing but our own faith and courage could help us.

Jim No, this seems to be a clear case of self-help or nothing, and I'm hanged if I can see what we can do.

Crispian Nor I—chained like this!

The sound of a trumpet is heard off up C. *Jim runs to the arch* C *and looks* **40** *off* L

Jim Look out! They're coming!

He moves quickly L. *Rosamund rises and runs to Jim. Crispian and Betty join them. Betty clings to Rosamund. Three Green Dragons and Three Red Dragons march on through the arch up* C. *They carry spears. They march down* C *then wheel* R *and form up each side of the throne. Dunks enters, backwards up* C, *bowing before the Dragon King who follows him on. The Dragon King is dressed in black armour. He smiles gloatingly as he sweeps past the children and mounts the rostrum and faces* L *as the Green and Red Dragons salute him. The whole of this is done with great ceremony.*

Dragons (*saluting*) Ya Goo!

Cubs enters up C *and rushes to the children grouped* L

Children (*ad lib*) Good old Cubs!
Dunks Silence!

Cubs turns, moves C *and faces the Dragon King*

Dragon King What is that?
Dunks The lion cub that was captured with the prisoners, your Majesty.
Dragon King Let him share their fate.

Cubs growls

(*to the children*) Prisoners, stand forth. (*He sits on his throne*)

Cubs moves one step forward. The children move and group C

You children stand guilty to the charge of daring to place yourselves under the protection of an ideal—one St George. Know then that ideals are the Dragon's greatest enemy. Where ideals are honoured our power is unknown: and this one in particular is here most hated: for he it is who ever foils my plans, and undermines my power and sovereignty. Therefore, what you have done is a capital offence, and the punishment (*he rises*) death.

Cubs growls. Betty and Rosamund cling together. Jim and Crispian stand defiant

(*He moves down* C, *stands with his back to the audience and faces the children*) The night is almost past—over the mountains soon the dawn will break—when you, one and all, will be cast headlong from the ramparts—to perish on the jagged rocks beneath. (*To Dunks*) Remove their fetters: for to the captive death is not so sharp as to the free.   **41**

Dunks crosses to Jim and Crispian and removes their fetters. The Red and Green Dragons form up and march off up C. *Dunks then bows to the Dragon King and exits up* C *taking the fetters with him. The Dragon King leaves his throne and crosses to the children, stands menacingly for a few moments over them. Jim and Crispian put their arms across Betty and Rosamund as though in protection. The Dragon King moves to the archway up* C, *turns, points to the ramparts* R *then with a gloating laugh, exits up* C. *Cubs runs to the archway and looks off* L *after him. Crispian moves down* RC *Rosamund eases* R. *Jim puts his arm round Betty*

Betty (*tearfully*) Must we really die, Jimmy?
Jim Yes. (*He sternly controls his emotion*) But you'll be brave, Betty, won't you?

Betty If Mummy only knew.

Crispian (*moving to* R *of Betty*) Oh, Betty, I was a brute to drag you into this.

Betty Oh, please don't mention it, Cris dear.

Jim (*easing* LC) If it's bad for Betty and me, it's worse for you two, just when you were on the point of finding your father and mother.

Rosamund Oh, that's kind of you, Blunders. And now—we've just—got—to—be brave—for their sakes.

Betty (*ruefully*) I don't expect they will ever know anything about it at home.

Crispian Never mind, they'll suffer for it sooner or later.

Cubs moves to R *of Betty*

Betty I'm not crying, of course, but I'm thinking how hard it is on poor old Cubs: he won't know why he is being killed.

Crispian I don't know. He looks as if he quite understood. (*To Cubs*) You'd sooner die than be a Dragon's pet, wouldn't you, Cubs?

Cubs nods his head and growls in agreement. The sound of measured footsteps is heard off up C

There, I said he knew! (*He glances up*) Ssh! Sentry.

The First Green Dragon, on sentry duty, appears in the arch from off L. *Cubs growls*

Jim Quiet, Cubs.

The First Green Dragon exits L

Rosamund runs up C, *looks off* L, *then moves to* L *of Crispian*

Rosamund (*with suppressed excitement*) Of course, it's a splendid thing to die bravely—and of course we will—unless——

Crispian Unless what?

Rosamund —we escape.

All (*ad lib*) Escape?

Rosamund Well, people generally do in books, you know. And when they're in quite as hopeless a fix as we are in.

Crispian (*in unconvinced tone*) Yes. So they do.

Rosamund I don't see why we should be more silly than anyone else, do you?

Jim No, why should we?

There is a pause

Crispian (*suddenly*) I know, let's all think hard.

Betty Yes. All think hard!

Crispian And the first one that has a brilliant idea—speak.

They all sit on the ground C *and face the audience; in order from* R *to* L—

Crispian, Rosamund, Betty, Cubs and Jim. They hold their heads. Cubs puts his right paw to his head and thinks. There is a pause

   (suddenly) By Jove! I have it! (*He rushes to the ramparts*)

The others all rise and rush to the ramparts

Jim
Rosamund } (*together, ad lib*) What? What?
Betty
Crispian (*very excitedly, but undecidedly*) You see . . . we might . . . if we could . . . But we couldn't.

They all sigh, return to their places and sit. Cubs puts his left paw to his head. There is a pause

Betty (*suddenly*) I know! (*She rises*) I know! (*she rushes excitedly to ramparts*)

The others all rise and rush to ramparts

Jim
Rosamund } (*together, ad lib*) What? What?
Crispian
Betty (*hesitantly*) You see, if we . . . No, that won't do.

They all sigh, return to their places and sit. Cubs puts both paws to his head. There is a pause, then an idea strikes Cubs. He rises, crosses below Betty to Rosamund and with a sharp whine tugs at his collar

Crispian (*pushing Cubs*) Be quiet, Cubs!

Cubs whines again

Rosamund Be quiet, Cubs, how can we think?

Cubs, very persistent, pulls at his collar, whines, and compels Rosamund to notice him. She looks at Cubs

   Why, I believe Cubs has thought of something.

Cubs tries frantically to remove his collar

   What is he doing? Oh, he wants me to take his collar off, poor old boy. (*She unfastens Cubs' collar*)

Cubs picks up the collar, waves it above his head, runs to the throne, puts the collar on the seat then sits below the rostrum very proudly

Jim What can he mean?
Crispian (*amused*) Why, he's captured the Dragon's throne.
Rosamund (*with sudden realization, very deliberately*) I know! I know what he means. We are to take this castle for St George!
Jim
Crispian } (*together; astounded*) But how?

They all rise

Rosamund (*after a glance round*) By pulling down the Dragon's flag and putting up St George's in its place. His flag once there, St George can help us.

Crispian You can't do it.

Rosamund No, *I* can't—you boys can.

Jim ⎫
Crispian ⎭ (*together*) We?

Rosamund Yes, you can climb. (*She points to the flagstaff on tower up* R) You see that flagstaff . . .

Jim Yes, but we haven't St George's flag!

Rosamund No, we must *make* one.

All Make one? How? How?

The First Green Dragon, on sentry duty, appears up C. *The children cluster together and scarcely dare to breathe. Cubs rises and growls. The first Green Dragon exits* L

Crispian (*the moment he has gone*) How, Rosamund?

Rosamund Quick, your handkerchief, Cris!

Crispian (*taking a large white handkerchief from his pocket and handing it to Rosamund*) My handkerchief? What's the good of that?

Rosamund (*running over to the rostrum of the throne*) Wait! (*She spreads the handkerchief on the rostrum*)

Jim, Crispian and Betty cluster around Rosamund. Cubs watches excitedly

Cubs' red ribbon! (*She takes the red bow from Cubs' collar and lays it on the handkerchief*)

Betty Cubs' red ribbon?

Crispian (*realizing Rosamund's scheme*) By Jove!

Rosamund (*kneeling by the rostrum*) Your knife, Cris!

Crispian takes his pocket-knife from his pocket

Cut it here.

Crispian cuts the ribbon in two

(*feels in her pocket*) I'm glad I brought those pins. (*She takes the packet of pins from her pocket*) Take these pins, Betty.

Betty and Rosamund pin the ribbon to the handkerchief in the form of a red cross. Cubs looks on excitedly

Crispian (*to Jim*) Blunders, you look out for the sentry.

Jim (*moving to the arch up* C) Right you are. (*He stands and looks off* L)

Rosamund More pins, Betty!

Betty Yes, yes.

Crispian Look, it sags in the middle.

Rosamund Another pin!

Jim (*calling*) Quick, he's turned.

Crispian Quick! Quick! More pins in the centre. Oh, take your nose out of it, Cubs! (*He pushes the eager Cubs away*)

Cubs rolls over. Although the flag must look as if it has been made out of the handkerchief and ribbon, Rosamund does not actually make it, but while the others are clustered round her, substitutes a flag previously concealed behind the step of rostrum

Betty Oh, hurry, hurry!
Jim (*calling*) Hurry up, he's coming!

Betty examines the flag, gives a shriek of delight and dances with excitement

Betty Lovely! Lovely!
Crispian Hush!

Rosamund rises and moves c

Rosamund Look! (*She holds up the flag*) The flag of St George!

The others all group around Rosamund

All (*ad lib*) Splendid! Splendid!
Jim (*in alarm*) The sentry! (*Moves to Crispian*)

The First Green Dragon appears up c *and glances suspiciously at the children, who look unconcerned. Rosamund conceals the flag behind her back*

Jim (*whispers to Crispian*) Are you ready, Cris?
Crispian Yes, when the sentry turns next time—*go.*
Jim Right you are!

The First Green Dragon moves down L. *The children stand breathless with excitement. The sound of a trumpet call is heard off up* L. *A pink glow appears in the sky and it starts to grow light.*
First Green Dragon It is the signal of the dawn.   **42**

He moves up c *and exits* L

Crispian runs up c. *Looks off* L *then runs to Rosamund*

Crispian *Now!*

He takes the flag from Rosamund and followed by Jim runs to the tower up R. *Crispian and Jim scramble up the ramparts and climb in at the window. Rosamund and Betty run* L. *Their excitement is intense. Cubs runs back and forth*

Rosamund⎱ (*ad lib*) Oh, hurry! Hurry!
Betty ⎰

The First Green Dragon enters up c *and looks suspiciously at the girls. He realizes that the boys are missing, runs to the girls and sees the boys climbing the tower. Cubs runs at the First Green Dragon*

First Green Dragon (*running towards the arch up* C *and calling*) Help! Help! The prisoners escape!

Cubs gets in the way and trips up First Green Dragon. There is a noise of shouting and a trumpet call off L. *The Red Dragons, followed by Dunks, run on up* C. *Dunks carries a drawn sword*

Dunks (*Up* C *calling*) Help! Help! The prisoners escape.

The Green Dragons, followed by the Dragon King enter up C. *The Dragon King carries a drawn sword. Jim and Crispian reach the top of the tower and commence to haul down the Dragon flag*

Dragon King (*up* C) What means this tumult?

Cubs runs to Rosamund and Betty and stands between them and the Dragon King to guard them

Dunks (*moving* LC) The prisoners escape, your Majesty! (*He points to the tower up* R)
Dragon King (*moving down* C) Escape? Impossible! (*He turns and looks up at the tower up* R)
Dunks See! They strike your Majesty's flag!

Jim throws the Dragon flag over the ramparts. He and Crispian hurriedly fix the St George's flag to the rope

One has something in his hand—they fasten it to the rope—
Dragon King (*with a yell of rage*) The Red Cross of St George! Quick! Drag the boys down—cast the girls from the ramparts ere the flag is hoisted and my power be gone!

The Red and Green Dragons seize Rosamund and Betty and drag them to the ramparts R. *the First Green Dragon makes his way to the top of the tower. Jim struggles with him and manages to tip him over the side of the tower. Just as the Dragons are about to throw the girls over the ramparts, Crispian runs up St George's flag in a frenzy of excitement. The moment the flag is hoisted, there is a flash of light, and St George, in brilliant armour, and with his drawn sword in his hand, appears on the ramparts up* R

St George Hold!
Rosamund ⎫
Betty ⎭ (*ad lib*) St George! St George!

The Dragons release Rosamund and Betty and cower away up L. *Jim and Crispian come down from the tower. Dunks moves down* L. *The Dragon King, a defiant, sinister figure, stands* C *and faces St George*

St George (*looking down on the Dragon King: sternly*) Once more we meet, arch-enemy, to fight the everlasting fight of good and evil. Foul tempter of mankind, I challenge thee to mortal combat!

Dragon King (*through clenched teeth*) Oh, ever-hated spoiler of my purpose —Champion of Christendom—to thee and thy cause do I and mine——

The Dragons shout menacingly

—vow eternal warfare and detestation.

St George (*with a loud cry*) Why then, lead on—(*He jumps from the ramparts and strides to* R *of the Dragon King*) For Freedom and the Right!

The Dragon King and St George engage in the fight. The children group up R. *Throughout the fight they urge on their champion with cries of* "St George!" *Cubs grabs his collar, climbs on to the ramparts and waves it excitedly. The fight is fierce, and at first, undecided. Thunder rolls and lightning flashes.*

The Dragons encourage their King with loud cries. St George is beaten to his knees, the Dragons cry out elated, but with a supreme effort St George parries the Dragon King's blow, and thrusting his sword aside, springs to his feet and closes with him again, driving him across to the foot of the throne. The Dragon King, who is tiring, makes a desperate lunge at St George, who, seeing his opportunity, thrusts his sword through the Dragon King's left side. With a cry, the Dragon King staggers back on to the throne, writhes a moment in a death agony, whilst St George stands on guard, watching him. Then, with a shudder, the Dragon King falls dead on to the throne. The moment the Dragons and Dunks see their King is dead, they slink silently away and exit up C. *The stage becomes flooded with light as the sun rises.*

The children, beside themselves with excitement, cluster around St George, who stands C. *Betty and Jim run* L *of him: Rosamund and Crispian* R *of him. Cubs runs down* L

St George (*lifts his sword in salute*) God for Freedom, Justice and the Right!

Rosamund⎫
Crispian ⎪ (*together: acclaiming St George*) St George! St George! St
Betty ⎬ George!
Jim ⎭

St George turns and points with his sword to sky back, where a rainbow appears

BLACK-OUT

Running TABS *close*

Rainbow children enter L *and walk across to* R. *They are dressed in short tunics and bare-footed.*

Rainbow Children (*singing*)
> Clouds left behind us, over the skies,

Rose, gold and blue the Rainbow bends.
The time of seeking's over,
  high our hopes ascend;
We'll find lost loved ones,
  we'll find lost loved ones,
United always in the land
  where the Rainbow Ends,
The Rainbow Ends.

The Rainbow Children exit R. *Will enters* L *leading Rosamund, Crispian, Betty, Jim and Cubs, and piping joyously. They cross to the* R *and exit* R

As the Tabs open the Rainbow Children enter L *playing and dancing and beckoning to each other, laughing happily*

SCENE 2

Where the Rainbow Ends and all lost loved ones are found   **43**

The scene depicts a lovely shore bathed in golden sunlight. The wings are of palm trees and flowers. The backcloth is a view over the sea with blue sky above; light tree-fringed cliffs R *and* L *and the arc of a Rainbow that loses itself in the shore. There is a ground row of low rocks across the stage, sufficiently below the backcloth to allow the passage across the stage above it of a boat truck*

As the Tabs open, the Rainbow Children move up stage. They dance, laugh happily, and play, some with a ball, others chasing each other

Rainbow Children (*singing*)
  Come and play along the sands;
  Play and dance and sing.
  All bright and gay is the laughing sea
  Bright is everything.
  All the year is may-time;
  All the year is Spring.
  Oh, 'tis always playtime,
  Time to dance and sing.
  Ah, sh . . .

Will enters R. *He runs to the middle of the stage where the Rainbow Children dance round him in a circle. Some try to catch him, but he eludes them and runs off* R. *He re-enters immediately and tells them, in mime, that a ship is approaching up* R. *He finishes down* L *where he stands waiting. All the Rainbow Children form into groups, waiting and looking up* R *expectantly. A boat in the form of a swan appears up* R. *Vera and Carey stand in the prow. When the boat reaches* C *Vera and Carey step out. They look hope-*

fully at the Rainbow Children, and, each taking one side, walk down among them, looking at each child in turn, eagerly searching their faces. They meet down C. *Vera looks despairingly at Carey. He sorrowfully shakes his head*

Carey (*tenderly*) You see, dearest—our children are not here.
Vera (*glancing sadly around*) Yet something seems to hold me here.
Carey Come, dearest. The ship is waiting for us. Believe me, our children are safe at home.

The children's voices are heard off R *in the distance, singing the "Rock-a-bye-Slumber" song*

Vera (*imploringly*) No, no—not yet . . .
Carey (*leading her slowly up* R) Vera, dearest, come.

The children's voices are heard singing nearer

Vera (*suddenly breaking from Carey and moving down* C) What's that? (*She listens intently*)

Carey moves down L

(*with a little cry*) Children's voices, singing. Don't you hear them?

Carey moves in to L *of Vera. The children's voices are now heard singing clearly*

(*with ecstasy*) It's Rosamund and Crispian! They are singing the song I sang to them when they were babies.

Carey grasps Vera's left hand in great emotion. They stand spellbound and look off R. *Rosamund and Crispian, followed by Jim, Betty and Cubs enter* R

Rosamund (*running to Carey*) Father!
Crispian (*running to Vera*) Mother!

Rosamund and Carey and Crispian and Vera embrace. Then Crispian embraces Vera, and Vera embraces Rosamund. Cubs capers round joyfully, then runs to Carey who lifts him up for a moment and hugs him. Crispian beckons to Jim and Betty who move to Vera and Carey and shake hands with them. Vera, Carey, Betty, Jim, Crispian, Rosamund and Cubs move up C *and all enter the boat. Cubs jumps in last of all. Will and the Rainbow Children wave farewell, and the boat moves off up* L *as*

the CURTAIN falls

EPILOGUE

When the CURTAIN *rises Carey, Vera, Jim, Crispian, Rosamund, Betty and Cubs are in the boat, with St George at the prow, resting on his sword*

The CURTAIN *rises and falls again*

St George is C *stage with Carey, Vera, Jim, Crispian, Rosamund, Betty and Cubs. Will and the Rainbow Children are grouped on the stage*

St George Dear Children—I hope you have enjoyed our play. Rosamund and Crispian have found their father and mother, and everyone is happy. But you know, all of you will have Dragon Woods to go through some time in your life, and you will meet people like the Slacker, who have given in and taken the easy way. Now I want you to promise me one thing—that when that time comes, whatever happens you'll be on the side of St George against the Dragon King. Now let me hear you all say "Yes! . . ." Oh, a *much* bigger "Yes!" than that! Now once again— one, two, three—"YES!" That's better!

       And now our tale is told, our play is done;
       We hope you have enjoyed it—every one.
       St George against the Dragon always stands,
       He calls upon the nations to take hands
       Shoulder to shoulder to redress
       All forms of misery and wickedness.
       Youth of all nations, pledge yourselves to fight,
       For Peace, for Justice, Freedom and the Right!

The National Anthem is sung

CURTAIN

FURNITURE AND PROPERTY PLOT

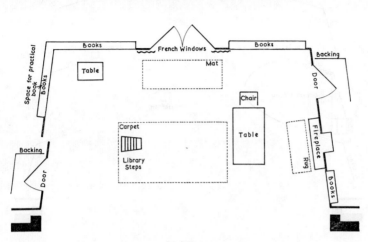

ACT I

On Stage: Large table. *On it:* cloth, table-lamp, length of clothes-line, **Crispian's**
cap
Small table. *On it:* bottle of medicine
Chair
Library steps. *On them:* book
Persian mat (with label under corner)
Fireside rug
On mantelpiece: clock, pair of candlesticks
Fire-irons
Fender
Carpet on floor
Bookcases with books
Persian and other curios
Other furniture as dressing
Pair of curtains and pelmet
Light switch above door down R
Electric pendant C

Set: *On floor up R of table* LC: packet of pins
Windows open
Window curtains open
Door down R closed
Door up L open
Table-lamp lit
Fire-on

Off Stage: Top-hat, whip (**Joseph**)

Personal: **Cubs:** collar with large red, white and blue ribbon
Matilda: scarf, handbag
Bertrand: inventory

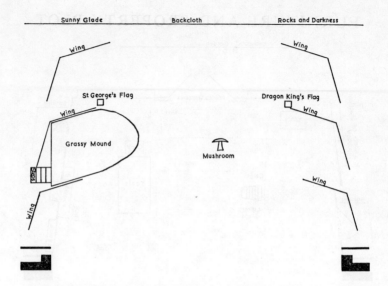

ACT II

On Stage: Grassy mound. *On it:* Persian mat, book, medicine bottle
Mushroom
2 Flagstaffs
Flag of **St George** R
Flag of **Dragon King** L
2 Electric fans

Off Stage: Broomstick **(Sea Witch)**
Dock-leaf. *On it:* strawberries **(Rosamund)**
Bundle of sticks **(Crispian)**
Bundle of sticks **(Jim)**

Personal: **Will-o'-the-Wisp:** reed pipe

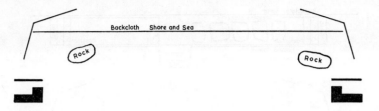

ACT III

SCENE 1

On Stage: 2 Rocks (RC and LC)

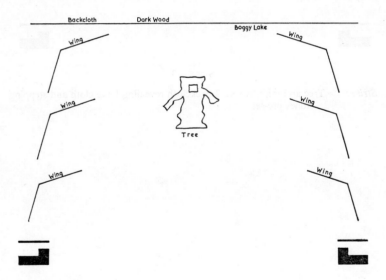

SCENE 2

On Stage: Hollow tree with operator

Personal: **Crispian:** handkerchief
Matilda: bag. *In it:* rope, gag

Off Stage: Lanterns (**Elves**)
Fishing-basket. *In it:* 2 apples (**Slacker**)

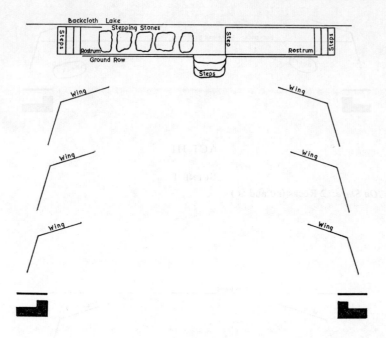

SCENE 3

Strike: Tree and raise SCENE 2 backcloth revealing Lake cloth and stepping
              stones pre-set

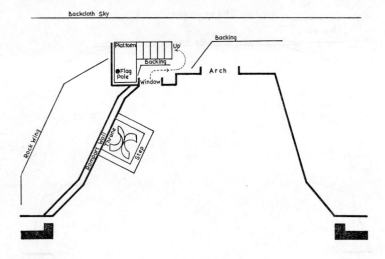

ACT IV

Scene 1

On Stage: Flagpole. *On it:* flag of the **Dragon King**
Electric fan
Throne on rostrum. *Concealed on the throne:* flag of **St George**

Off Stage: Fetters for **Crispian** and **Jim**
Spears for **Dragons**

Personal: **Betty:** handkerchief
Crispian: large white handkerchief, pocket-knife
Rosamund: packet of pins
Dragon King: sword
Dunks: sword

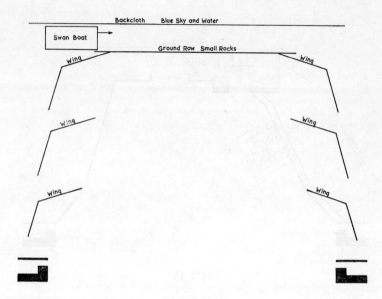

SCENE 2

Off Stage: Swan boat

LIGHTING PLOT

Property fittings required for Act I: Table-lamp, centre pendant. Switches above
    door down R. Fire in grate
Flash device

ACT I. The library. Night

The apparent source of light are an electric pendant C, a table-lamp on the table
    LC and bright moonlight outside the windows up C
The Main Acting Area is C

To open: Table-lamp switched on
              Fire on
              Pendant C out

Cue 1   **Rosamund** switches on pendant C   (Page 2)
             Bring up lights C. *Switch on pendant* C

Cue 2   **William** switches out table-lamp and pendant C   (Page 9)
             Check all lights except the fire and moonlight. Switch out pendant and
             table-lamp

Cue 3   **Rosamund:** "Oh, Carpet's Genie, now appear"   (Page 9)
             Bring in blue light to cover mat up C

Cue 4   **William:** ". . . I must watch this!"   (Page 9)
             Fade out blue light on mat up C

Cue 5   **Rosamund** switches on table-lamp   (Page 9)
             Bring up lights to cover LC. *Switch on table-lamp*

Cue 6   **Rosamund:** "Oh, Carpet's Genie, now appear."   (Page 10)
             Bring in blue light to cover mat up C

Cue 7   **Rosamund:** ". . . and I ask your aid."   (Page 14)
             Flash R

Cue 8   **St George:** ". . . Justice and the Right!"   (Page 15)
             Black-out

Cue 9   After **St George's** exit   (Page 16)
             Bring in lights as they were prior to the black-out

Cue 10   **William** waves piece of carpet   (Page 16)
             Black-out

Cue 11   **William** switches on pendant C   (Page 17)
             Bring up lights C, *moonlight and fire. Switch on pendant* C

Cue 12   **Joseph:** "Never—never—never!"   (Page 18)
             Bring in red glow

ACT II. The outskirts of the Dragon's Wood. Late afternoon

The Main Acting Areas are R and RC

To open: The lighting R and RC is bright
              The lighting L and LC is dim
              Sunset effect on backcloth

Cue 13   At rise of CURTAIN *all lights check slowly as the sun sets. Continue to*
             the end of the Act   (Page 19)

Cue 14   **Joseph:** ". . . fetch you back again!"   (Page 28)
             Flash R

Cue 15   **St George** *exits* R   (Page 28)
             Flash R

ACT III SCENE 1. The Witch's Cove. Sunset

Cue 16   **Will** and **Vera** exit L   (Page 34)
             Black-out

ACT III SCENE 2. The Dragon's Wood. Evening

Cue 17   **Elves** enter with lanterns   (Page 35)
             Increase lights

Cue 18   **Elves** exit with lanterns   (Page 36)
             Check lights

Cue 19   The **Black Bear** sits and laughs   (Page 45)
             Black-out

ACT III SCENE 3. The Lake at the end of the Wood. Night

Cue 20   **Crispian:** ". . . give you a hand, Betty?"   (Page 47)
             Commence slow dim of all lights. Continue to end of Scene

Cue 21   For CURTAIN   (Page 47)
             Silhouette effect on the **Dragon King**

ACT IV SCENE 1. The ramparts of the Dragon's castle. Night

Cue 22   Trumpet call   (Page 48)
             *Commence pink glow on sky and slow rise of all lights. Continue until
               end of Scene*

Cue 23   **St George** enters R   (Page 54)
             Flash R

Cue 24   **St George** and **Dragon King** fight   (Page 55)
             Lightning flashes during fight

Cue 25   The **Dragon King** dies   (Page 55)
             Bring up all lights to full sunshine

ACT IV SCENE 2. Where the Rainbow Ends. Golden Sunlight.
             No cues

LIMES PLOT

ACT I
No cues

ACT II

Cue 1	**Will-o'-the-Wisp** enters L *Follow* **Will**	(Page 21)
Cue 2	**Will** exits L *Off*	(Page 21)

ACT III SCENE 1

Cue 3	**Will** enters R *Follow* **Will**	(Page 33)
Cue 4	**Will** exits L *Off*	(Page 34)
Cue 5	**Will** enters R *Follow* **Will**	(Page 35)
Cue 6	**Will** exits L *Off.*	(Page 35)

ACT III SCENE 2

Cue 7	**Slacker** enters R *Follow* **Slacker** *with green light*	(Page 37)
Cue 8	**Jim:** "Of course not!" *Start fade of green light on* **Slacker**	(Page 39)
Cue 9	**Jim:** ". . . we've done our best." *Switch off green light on* **Slacker**	(Page 39)
Cue 10	**Slacker:** ". . . to starve—*never!*" *Bring in green light on* **Slacker**	(Page 39)
Cue 11	**Slacker** exits L *Off*	(Page 39)
Cue 12	**Will** *enters* L *Follow* **Will**	(Page 40)
Cue 13	**Will** exits L *Off*	(Page 41)

ACT III SCENE 3

Cue 14	**Will** enters *Follow* **Will**	(Page 46)
Cue 15	**Will** *exits* R *Off*	(Page 46)

ACT IV SCENE 1
No cues

ACT IV SCENE 2
No cues

MAGICAL EFFECTS

On stages where the use of a trap is not possible, the entrances of the **Genie** (page 10) and the **Dragon King** (page 18) can be made through the french windows, their appearances being covered by a Black-out and a flash.

At the end of Act I the **Dragon King** can exit majestically through the windows, **Joseph** following, and **Matilda,** very scared, allowing **Bertrand** to lead her; a puff of smoke and a red glow outside the windows complete the effect.